THE THIRD LAW

TAMRA RYAN, CEO
WOMEN'S BEAN PROJECT

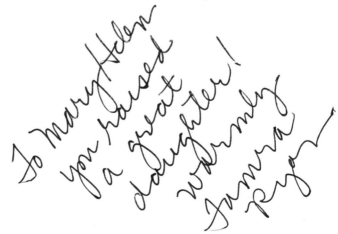

To mary Helen
you raised
a great
daughter!
warmly
Tamra
Ryan

GILPIN HOUSE PRESS

This book is dedicated to all women who are working to create a better life for themselves and their families.

A portion of the proceeds from this book will create an emergency revolving loan fund for Women's Bean Project program participants and graduates. Women will have the opportunity to apply for emergency funding for utility bills, housing deposits, prescription drug refills, pressing dental needs, or other expenses that, if not addressed, risk taking the women off-track.

THE THIRD LAW

Copyright© *2013 by Tamra Ryan*

Print ISBN: 978-0-9899190-0-5   EISBN: 978-0-9899190-1-2

Library of Congress Control Number: 2013950007

Third Law is a book of nonfiction. The names of all
program participants and graduates in this book have been changed.

Cover and Interior Design: Cindi Yaklich Epicenter Creative, LLC
Cover Photography: PhotoAlto/Alix Minde/Getty Images

TABLE OF CONTENTS

INTRO	Why the Third Law?	6
CHAPTER 1	Whac-a-Mole... Facing the pressure to change	14
CHAPTER 2	Culture Clash... How I learned to step beyond my suburban, middle-class roots	36
CHAPTER 3	Two Steps Forward, Three Steps Back... How poverty self-perpetuates	53
CHAPTER 4	Freedom's Just Another Word... How the criminal justice system works against rehabilitation	79
CHAPTER 5	The Devil You Know... Why domestic violence is so hard to escape	103
CHAPTER 6	There but for the Grace of God... Why the women are their own worst enemies	123
CHAPTER 7	Chickens and Eggs... How mental illness, drug use and poverty intersect	139
CHAPTER 8	First Comes Baby... Why motherhood is nearly impossible to avoid	150
CHAPTER 9	The Ties That Bind... How families help, hinder and perpetuate	163
CHAPTER 10	Relapse... Why drugs are so seductive	184
CHAPTER 11	The Women and Their Crimes... Fighting the bias against felons	204
CHAPTER 12	There Was a Thief... How appearances deceive	217
CHAPTER 13	Orientation Day... Why employment is the solution	230
CHAPTER 14	Beautiful Boy...When my life and work collided	239
EPILOGUE	Now what?	265

WHY THE THIRD LAW?

I like things to be in compartments. My sock drawer displays each pair folded into thirds and filed according to color. My spice cabinet is alphabetized. Chaos is fine as long as I can assess the situation, develop a plan and put things in order relatively quickly.

Putting things in order relatively quickly was exactly what I set out to do when I became CEO of Women's Bean Project in 2003. Women's Bean Project—or the Bean, as it is sometimes called–is a place where chronically unemployed and impoverished women come for a second chance in life. Most of the women who arrive at the Bean Project have never held a job longer than a year. They are convicted felons, recovering addicts, victims of domestic violence. Many were teenage mothers and high school dropouts. They come to Women's Bean Project for a chance to create new lives out of the rubble theirs have become.

Founded in 1989, the Bean Project is an anomaly in the business world. It is a business, one that packages and sells bean soup mixes and other food products to stores across the country. We also have a business that makes handmade jewelry. But tucked inside these businesses is a human services organization designed to provide a safe and accepting work environment where impoverished women can learn the skills required for gainful employment.

When I was hired as CEO, the Bean faced several daunting challenges. The year before, it had struggled through a financial crisis that almost caused it to close. While the board and an interim director kept the doors open with various emergency measures, including releasing most of the staff, the problems that led to the crisis had not been addressed. Armed with two science degrees and a fifteen-year career in business marketing, I felt qualified to tackle those challenges. My focus would be on increasing sales and marketing, boosting production, cutting costs and raising profits. I could do this, I thought. No problem. I was excited by the potential.

I couldn't have been more naive.

What I didn't recognize were the human challenges involved in running a business whose employees were the neediest among us. I hadn't thought about why our employees might not have held a job for longer than a year. I had no idea that even if a woman tried with all her might to change her life, there were powerful forces pushing back on her attempts to change. The culture I stepped into at the Bean Project couldn't have been more different from my own white, middle-class, suburban upbringing — a fact I soon confronted.

During my first week at the Bean Project, in an attempt to learn the business, I was working on the bean soup production line with a woman named Fadilah. Because we were standing so close, I started asking questions to break the ice and become acquainted. "How did you end up here, Fadilah?" I asked, while scooping beans from staging bins into long, plastic sleeves.

"When I was fourteen, I started selling drugs," she said. "It was fast money, easy money. Everyone I knew was using, so I could sell to them and support my son and my little brother." Fadilah was fourteen when she had her son, while she also was caring for her ten-year-old brother because her mother was one of Fadilah's drug customers.

While listening to Fadilah, I thought about what I was doing at fourteen. I had just started running track and my 4x200 relay team qualified for a national meet, in West Virginia. It would be my first airplane trip and I was able to go without my parents.

"Didn't you want your son to grow up in a better environment than you, with your mom using and you being surrounded by drugs?" I asked, as though there had been a menu of choices, and Fadilah had chosen selling drugs over, say, going to the high school prom or taking AP English. I'm embarrassed now, but this is how I thought back then. I thought people who got in trouble with the law were bad people who made poor choices. People who committed crimes and took drugs got what they deserved. If we could catch them and lock them away, our communities would be safer, crime would decline and drug use would decrease.

As someone who grew up with a lot of opportunity, I believed that anything was possible in America. Therefore, poor people, unwed teenage mothers and high-school dropouts clearly were responsible for their own misery since they hadn't taken advantage of the choices available to them. I believed that if we worked hard, society worked with us to help us succeed.

I believed that Fadilah had consciously chosen one life over another. In reality, the only choice she made was survival. She chose to make the situation work for her based on what she knew.

She had no one in her life to help her see that selling drugs would lead her down a path of destruction and eventually take her away from all that she held dear.

It was easy for me to think this way because I had never met any of the people I judged so harshly. I was a well-educated but clueless white girl who led from the head, not the heart. I believed that life is a manifestation of the choices we make. Conveniently, all my choices were condoned by my community.

My perspective changed the moment I set foot inside Women's Bean Project and met the women we employed.

I met Chalina, whose mother introduced her to cocaine when she was twelve and then kicked her out of the house because she saw Chalina as competition for boyfriends. Chalina landed on the streets to fend for herself until she was eighteen and was arrested and incarcerated for drug manufacturing.

I met Waseme, who struggled with PTSD from a street assault and suffered from a debilitating bipolar disorder. I watched firsthand as she cycled from being a delightful, bubbly young woman to someone who couldn't get out of bed when she didn't have the money for her mood-stabilizing medication.

I met Sharifa, who at twenty-one was charged with first-degree murder for killing the fiancé who had been beating her for six years. Though convicted of involuntary manslaughter, she received an extremely harsh twenty-six-year sentence. After Sharifa had served seven years, the judge released her, asked if she had learned her lesson, and sent her to the halfway house, her home while she worked at the Bean Project.

Slowly, but steadily, I learned that the circumstances faced by our employees had not come about because they had chosen incorrectly, but because they had no role models for employment, no one pushing them to stay in school, no one discouraging them from getting pregnant as teens. They were disenfranchised from the community in every sense. Most were victims who had been further victimized by drug sentencing laws, cultural prejudices and human services systems that dehumanized them. In short, I learned that it's society that holds certain women back.

But I also learned about something far more moving: the resiliency of the human spirit. I met countless women at the Bean Project who faced and overcame insurmountable odds. They taught me that it is possible to confront and overcome fear and shame and lack of self-worth. I have seen how difficult, but necessary, it is to stare adversity in the eye. And despite setbacks—because setbacks always occur—a path to a new life can be created. I have seen for myself the value and impact of a woman believing she is worthy of a better life.

When I began writing this book, I thought the question was "How do we do what we do at the Bean Project? How do we change lives?" But I began to see this wasn't the point at all.

Newton's Third Law of Motion says that for every action there is an equal and opposite reaction. Applied to physics, this means that for every force there is a reaction that is equal in size, but opposite in direction. For the women at the Bean Project, this means that even as they try to create new lives for themselves, by doing just what society asks of them—get a job, pay taxes, support their children— a myriad of forces conspire to push back against their progress.

These opposing forces exist in our biases and prejudices against felons, addicts and welfare recipients. They exist within the human services systems that cut benefits while a woman works to create a foundation to decrease her dependence on just those services. The forces exist within the corrections system that creates barriers to success and demeaning methods for keeping convicted felons in line.

In truth, society is not entirely to blame, because I also have seen these women work against themselves. On the brink of success, they self-sabotage through passive-aggressive behavior, relapse or other choices that return them to prison. Low self-esteem makes it hard for them to believe in their worthiness for employment outside of the Bean Project. Their addictive backgrounds stand in their way of finding healthy, productive strategies for dealing with life's challenges.

Families also are a force working against women at the Bean. The codependence found in a household mired in addiction can undermine even the most committed recovering addict. In a family life where chaos is the norm, the creation of a calm, orderly life is elusive. Women whose parents were addicts don't know what a "normal" childhood is and often re-create dysfunction in their own families, ranging from poor parenting skills to drug use and criminal behavior. By the time they come of age, their kids are poised to make the same mistakes, pulling their mothers down with them.

The Third Law has even affected me. As CEO of Women's Bean Project, I lead a system that exerts pressure on these women to change. In return, opposing forces from the women have caused me to change. I have moved from being a hard-hearted, business-focused woman to being someone who wants—no, needs—to know each woman's story. Fundamentally, in ways I never could have imagined, I have changed.

Although I didn't know it at the time, I had many prejudices when I walked through the doors of Women's Bean Project. But it was more than that—I had little awareness of those prejudices, how they'd formed and why. I had never really thought about what I believed because my beliefs had never been challenged. While getting to know the women of the Bean, I got to know myself. With this new awareness I've found compassion and understanding. I have developed an ability to empathize with women on a level I would have never thought possible.

I used to believe the world was black and white. Right or wrong. Good or bad. Today I understand there are thousands of gray shades in between. It was one thing to judge women whom I'd never met. It has been something else entirely getting to know these women one by one, to look into their eyes and feel the pain in their stories. With this awareness, there is no room to judge. I have cried for joy with the women, as proud as any mother of their accomplishments. I have felt deep sympathy for their trials, often driving home at night wondering if there were other ways I could help. I have mourned their losses, hugging my own children while reflecting on the children they lost. I have also felt anger, disappointment and sadness when women at the Bean make choices that take them backward.

When I first meet women who come to Women's Bean Project, I see anger and hurt. I see closed-up women who are afraid to imagine anything better for their lives. And yet, they arrive at the Bean Project hoping for a chance, that maybe this will be the program that changes everything. The women at the Bean have nothing left to lose and their lives to re-gain.

The stories I most want to tell are those of the women themselves—women who, against all odds, have turned their lives around. Too often, they buy into the notion that society puts in front of them: that they aren't good enough—to be hired by an employer who will care about them, to earn enough money to finally move off of assistance, to have a life they and their children can be proud of. At times like this, I want to grab these women by the hand, pull them along and show the world the women I have come to know. The women in this book have taken what life has presented them, some of it their own making, much of it not, and created a mess that they are working to correct. My hope is that by sharing their stories of struggle, survival and, sometimes, triumph, I will give these women a voice. By illustrating our communities' social ills, I hope to draw out the compassion required to support these women. Finally, it is my hope that this book, by illuminating the cycle of poverty and chronic unemployment, might stimulate readers to act differently, hire differently, vote differently and give differently.

This book is a story with no end. There will always be chronically unemployed women, a system that works against them, and opinions and attitudes that undermine their success. In the same way that women at the Bean Project become empowered to take responsibility for their actions, so can we, as taxpayers and voters, begin to take responsibility for our influence on the laws and policies that trap individuals and families in some of our societies' most intractable intergenerational social ills.

CHAPTER 1

WHAC-A-MOLE—
FACING THE PRESSURE TO CHANGE

It was June 2003 and I had just been named CEO of Women's Bean Project. I was sitting at my desk, wrapping up some loose ends at my former job when the phone rang. It was the deputy director of the Bean Project calling on behalf of Maude, the production supervisor. At the time there was no production manager and Maude was responsible for all aspects of manufacturing. The deputy director was letting me know that they had received a big order—one that would bring in much-needed sales revenue, and, while she knew they didn't have enough beans to complete the order, no one had any idea how many more beans were needed. Could I come over and help figure it out?

It seemed odd. How could they have gotten through fourteen years of operations as a bean soup manufacturer without knowing how many beans are needed to make a bag of soup mix?

I drove to the Bean Project during my lunch break and sat down with Maude and the deputy director at the end of a long conference table. Maude smiled a lot. Her long hair was pulled back from her large, round face and gathered up in a hairnet; she'd just come from working on the production line. Both women leaned forward, waiting for me to begin, so I rapidly reverted to basic algebra. "For every fifty pound bag of beans, how many bags of soup can be created?"

Awkward silence. No one knew the answer. I could see in Maude's blank look that she was very much over her head. I knew Maude was a program graduate, and I later learned that while she excelled at supervising and communicating with the program participants, she had poor reading and math skills, possibly the result of a learning disability. She didn't have a high school diploma or her General Equivalency Diploma (GED). I was told that earning a GED wasn't a realistic goal for her; she didn't have the capacity.

We didn't accomplish much during that lunch hour. I tried to help them figure out how many bags of beans they needed to order, but I don't think I was very useful. After I went back to my office, they were so desperate to ensure they had enough beans and so anxious about spending money that they sorted the beans from the seconds bin.

The seconds bin is a large, round industrial container, resembling a janitorial trashcan. Whenever a bag splits during production or a soup mix is made incorrectly, the beans are poured en masse into the seconds bin, where the beans get mixed up in a collage of colors. Though the beans and spices are the same, soup mixes made from the seconds bin are sold at a discount because they do not contain the beautiful, earth-toned layers that are a distinguishing feature of Women's Bean Project's soups.

A few months into my tenure at the Bean I discovered there were calculators that enabled someone to plug-in the number of finished units of soup needed, subtract what was on hand, and calculate the required raw materials. Even if Maude had known they existed, I'm not sure she would have had the ability to use them. One problem solved while the list of other issues grew. I began writing in a notebook all of the challenges the business faced, even if I didn't have a solution. I thought of it as my "worry book." I reasoned that as long as my concerns were documented in the notebook, I could set them aside until there was time to fix them or a solution was found. It didn't take long before I realized the notebook was going to have many entries and my job was going to be much more challenging than I'd thought. I only hoped I was up to the task.

I was attracted to Women's Bean Project because I thought the business was intriguing. How fascinating, I thought when I first learned about the organization. They make soup and they help women. I wondered how the two could work together but loved the idea nonetheless. The notion that the better the business performed, the more women could be helped enhanced my interest.

My involvement with the Bean Project began about eight months before I became CEO, when I was asked to volunteer on its sales and marketing committee. My introduction to the Bean Project was a meeting with Judy, the acting CEO, and Susan, the board chair. At the time, I didn't know enough to ask why there was an acting CEO. It didn't occur to me that perhaps there were some issues, and I was too inexperienced to know what questions to ask.

I was hooked after my first visit to the building. When I approached the two-story, iron-red brick building for the first time, I noted its historical significance. "1928 Denver Fire Department Station #10" was embedded in the brick above the three bay doors out of which the fire trucks once rushed toward their rescues. The ivy-colored entrance door sat under a miniature awning, creating a quaint entry.

Inside, I was welcomed by the aroma of cumin, curry, oregano and the other fragrant spices used in the gourmet food products. I was lucky to arrive on a day when they were baking oatmeal chocolate chip cookies. The scent of the freshly baked cookies wafted from the kitchen and blended seamlessly with the spices. I made a mental note to stop at the retail store on my way out to make a few purchases.

As I walked across the first floor to the stairs, I noted the positive vibe and good-natured energy coming from the women working on the food production line. Their laughter combined with the din of the radio and the rhythm of beans being placed, one scoop at a time, into packages. As I walked past, I was greeted graciously by program participants. They seemed to be trying to ensure that every person who entered Women's Bean Project knew how special it was.

Upstairs on the second floor was an open area with warmly refinished hardwood floors flooded with natural light. The building was an old-time fire station, right down to the holes in the floor, where poles used to transport firemen from their slumber to their fire truck, lickety-split and ready for action. Banks of the old wooden firemen's lockers were in their original positions along the walls, adding to the charm.

In Judy's office, during that first visit, I noticed piles of paper strewn about but didn't connect them to chaos. She was a kind-faced woman, with silver-gray hair and soft blue eyes who frequently hesitated when speaking, as if she struggled to choose the right words. We talked around those piles of paper just as we talked around the organizational problems that soon became so apparent.

As I began to volunteer, I learned much more about Women's Bean Project, including the financial crisis with which it struggled. I recall sitting in frequent, somber meetings with Judy and other board members looking at the details of cash flow, inventory, donations and sales. It quickly became clear that helping this organization required much more than just sitting on the sales and marketing committee. The organization was down to bare-bones staff. Every penny counted, and there were many references to requesting help from foundations to keep the operations afloat. Yet I saw so much potential. Women's Bean Project is a marketer's dream come true. Stories of the women, their lives and their journeys were everywhere, and on each of the products was a surface on which those stories could be told. My first observation was that there were many, many missed opportunities for telling the Bean Project story, not for lack of desire, but just from not knowing how. I rolled up my sleeves and volunteered in earnest, excited about giving my time where I thought I would be able to see the results of the work and benefit the organization.

About six months later, in the spring of 2003, the position of CEO came open when Judy determined that it was time for her to move on and for the organization to find permanent leadership. I immediately thought of my friend Sarah as the perfect leader of the Bean Project. Sarah had worked in the nonprofit sector so I made my best sales effort to convince her that the Bean Project would be a cool job. Finally Sarah said, "If you think it's so great, then why don't you do it?"

I quickly responded, "Oh, no, I'm not a nonprofit person." Applying for the position had never occurred to me.

Sarah responded, "It's not a nonprofit; it's a business."

"Well, the salary is quite a bit lower than I currently make." In fact, it was forty percent less than I was earning at that time.

"How much money do you need?" Sarah challenged.

I had never thought about a salary that way, having always measured my professional progress, at least in part, by my progression up the pay scale. Our conversation nagged at me for several days. Was there a way to combine personal and professional fulfillment?

I had two science degrees and used them in minor ways throughout my career, but I mostly had followed whatever interesting professional opportunities I encountered. I felt fulfilled by work because it was intellectually challenging and financially rewarding, and I got to travel the world. I'd grown up in a home where a job was a job. My father was a laborer and, as I recall, often out of work with the ebbs and flows of the economy. After their divorce, my mom struggled to return to the workforce at a wage that would enable her to support a household with four children. By earning an advanced education, I had improved my lot over my parents', but I carried baggage that manifested in my making sure I always could support myself. I needed to prove I could thrive all on my own.

I liked the idea of becoming a CEO. I felt I was at a point in my career where I wanted to run something. I wanted to be in charge, make the hard decisions and shape the strategy of the company. All these notions were very abstract, but they seemed like the responsibilities of a CEO. I'd had a few experiences in which I had disagreed with the strategy, decisions or style of the CEO at companies where I worked. Maybe this was my chance to be the CEO I'd always hoped others would be.

The more I thought about it, the more I began to picture myself in the position. I was both nervous and inspired when I finally decided to apply for the job. I thought I had the skills to lead an organization, but I didn't know for sure.

At the time, when I imagined leadership, I pictured myself saying in my best cheerleader voice, "Hey, everybody! Let's take the organization in this direction! Yeah, I know it seems like it will be hard, but we can do it if we all work together!" I wanted to be different from leaders who did not inspire me. I'd worked under CEOs who used intimidation, authority and threats to get what they wanted. I just wanted to be inspired. I knew I was always going to work hard, but I wanted the leaders to paint a clear picture of the larger purpose so I could feel good about the purpose behind our efforts.

In selecting me, someone coming from an entirely different world, with no proven experience running a nonprofit organization, or any organization, Susan and the other board members made a huge leap of faith. In the end, they said my background in business was exactly what they were seeking because they thought that the issues of the organization were related to how the business was run. None of us had any idea that the skills required were ones I had yet to develop.

During my first week at the Bean Project I thought it was important to get a better sense of how the products were made. On my second or third day, I started by watching the bean soup production line. After a bit, I decided it was time to don a hairnet and latex gloves and jump into the action. We were making Toni's Ten Bean Soup, our original product, which has remained the Bean Project's bestseller. Surprisingly, assembling each bag of soup required a bit of a balancing act. The women enthusiastically showed me how to hold each bag with a plastic funnel inside with one hand and a quarter-cup scoop in the other. Then, they coached me on holding the funnel-bag combination with just the right amount of pressure to avoid losing the bag when the beans were added. Starting from the far left of two end-to-end, hip-high, stainless steel production tables, I stood in front of the first bin of beans. Each scoop had to be filled level, not mounded, before being added to the bag. After emptying each scoop into the bag, we shifted a few inches to the right to position in front of the next bin of beans. Within a few minutes we got into the rhythm of the scooping to "Ain't Too Proud to Beg" broadcast from the Motown station that had been selected that morning. Arriving at the exact weight was not as easy as it appeared from the sidelines. It required some trial and error to determine how full each scoop needed to be to reach the final weight without adding or subtracting a few beans at the end. We hummed and swayed to the music, pouring into the bag, scooping the next bean, pouring into the bag. Nine different times I scooped and poured.

"Wait. Shouldn't there be ten beans in Toni's Ten Bean Soup?" I asked. Was I missing something? Was this intentional?

I wasn't missing something; something was missing. No one had noticed that only nine bins had been brought out and filled with beans that day, and no one seemed bothered by the mistake. I explained that one of the crazy things about food manufacturing is that the list of ingredients on the label actually has to match the contents list on the packaging. Every package of nine bean soup we had made had to be emptied into the seconds bin, I said. It hit a few of the women that all their work that morning had been futile.

Nonplussed, a short, red-haired woman asked, "We'll make more this afternoon, right? Well, we'll do it right then."

How can a business operate successfully when a half day's work is for naught?

Another time, we made a large batch of brownie mix to fill an order to be sent to a few hundred clients of one of our corporate customers. We also sent a few bags from the batch to a catalog that carried our soups, hoping they might add our brownies to their offering. A few days after the brownies arrived at their intended destinations, Geoff, our sales manager, began receiving calls. Customers said our brownies were salty. Initially, we thought customers may have used salted butter in baking the mix. Really, how salty could they be? Finally there were too many complaints so we removed a package from the warehouse and baked it ourselves. The finished product looked great; chocolaty, crispy-flaky on top, with just the right amount rise. My love of chocolate generally puts me at the front of the line for brownie taste-testing. Eagerly, I took a bite and a bizarre taste sensation overtook my mouth. The taste matched neither the appearance nor the expectation I had for brownies. Those beautiful, chocolaty brownies were salty!

With some rapid investigation, we discovered that while we'd been making that batch, sugar and salt had been switched. It was an expensive mistake. We replaced the brownies for the corporate customer, but that was their last order with us. It took several years before the catalog company gave us another chance and finally began carrying the brownie mix—made properly.

A quick investigation revealed the problem. Anita, the woman who had mixed the ingredients that day, was, at best, marginally literate. I was confused. Anita, Maude, the production supervisor, and I sat down together at the big stainless steel table in the kitchen, the original scene of the brownie debacle. Over the hum of the commercial refrigerator and freezer, we began asking about her process for mixing the batch. After several minutes, she timidly shared that, as she looked over the recipe, she tried to match the word on the recipe with the labels on the raw ingredients. Since sugar and salt both began with ''s, she had become confused and lost track of how much of each the recipe called for. I knew Anita was a great cook. How did she manage if she couldn't follow a recipe?

"Oh, I never follow recipes. My mother taught me everything about cooking. Everyone loved her food." She smiled broadly.

"Anita, if you can't read, how do you know which bus to take or what the street signs say?" I asked, trying to comprehend how she functioned in the community. I knew we occasionally sent Anita to the grocery store down the street to buy baking supplies or other items. "How do you know what the labels at the grocery store say, or how much something costs?"

"You don't need to know how to read to get around. I just remember everything. I grew up here in Denver and I remember the streets. I know the bus routes I need. I don't have to read." The idea of reading labels at the grocery sounded silly to her. "Why would I do that? I know what to buy when I look at the packages."

How can a business be successful with expensive mistakes and illiterate employees?

One day, during my first holiday season, I worked with Louise in the shipping department. Louise never said much to her co-workers, but she wasn't unfriendly, merely quiet. Her manner was slow and deliberate, the result of methadone, a non-addictive heroin replacement. Methadone treatment is used to prevent withdrawal symptoms and replace the desire for heroin.

We were in the middle of holiday season, and the orders were piling up. To speed up fulfillment, we both were assembling shipping boxes. I enjoy this kind of work; rolling up my sleeves and making the same motions over and over again felt Zen-like in the middle of the holiday chaos. Fold, press the sides to the middle, tape the middle, tape the one side, tape the other side. Voila! I got a system down and assembled fifteen or so boxes before I looked over at Louise. In that same time, she barely had put together one box. With a pleasant look on her face, she focused on each motion, but it appeared as though she was swimming through Jell-O. I didn't know if her dosage needed adjusting or if that was what it was like on methadone. I couldn't imagine how she functioned in any aspect of her life, because she definitely wasn't high functioning at work.

How can a business be successful when the employees are, by definition, impaired?

I suspect people sometimes wonder how it's possible that the Bean Project continues to make mistakes after years of claiming it is making continuous improvements. I imagine they ask behind our backs, "Don't they ever learn?" We do learn. Every January, at the first staff meeting of the year, we do a postmortem. To that meeting we each bring our laundry lists of what worked during the prior holiday season and what didn't. We hold this meeting soon after the New Year, while the discomfort from the holidays is still fresh. That list—of mistakes and processes poorly executed—becomes our work plan for the next several months. Before the next holiday season, we tweak and revamp when everyone is motivated to make changes because no one ever wants a reprise of the prior year.

But then, when the next holiday season arrives, along with a new group of program participants and some invariable staff turnover, more challenges find their way to the surface, as in a Whac-a-Mole game. We're fortunate; our customers are forgiving. Our volunteers tell us they love being needed when we rally them to create extra production shifts to help meet our product demands. It seems to me we should be able to solve some of our problems. And yet we don't.

Despite what I may have originally thought, the Bean Project is not a particularly good business model. There is a constant tension between the business and the mission. I have come to enjoy this tension, learning that some days the business wins and other days the program wins. There may be a day in December when we focus entirely on getting orders out the door, jamming into the production and shipping departments. In the slower summer months, several hours in a day may be spent in a computer skills class. On balance, we do the best we can. We hire the most difficult employees, those whom no one else will hire or those struggling to move from welfare to work, and we attempt to make them employable. Once they learn to come to work, become reliable, and develop better communication skills, we help them transition to other jobs in the community where those employers reap the benefits of our efforts.

We hire women who aren't able to prioritize, who struggle with paying attention to details, whose lives are such a mess that merely coming to work—going anywhere consistently and on time—is a challenge.

Women's Bean Project is, by definition, transitional employment. The program provides short-term employment (six to twelve months) augmented by skill development and support services designed to help participants get and keep a job. Transitional jobs are a way to bring people into mainstream, unsubsidized employment. The work we do at the Bean is aimed at helping women overcome the most significant barriers to employment, including little or no work experience; low education and skill levels; criminal backgrounds; and health, housing and child care issues. We hire the women whom no one else will hire, and we try to run an effective business that serves to give them a second chance and provide us the ability to pay them.

A typical woman who applies to work at the Bean Project has never held a job longer than a year, and the average age of our workforce is thirty-eight. During her employment, she must learn to come to work every day and on time. In my first year, one woman was averaging about 30 percent attendance. When our case manager spoke with her, she said, "I thought this was a program. I didn't know I needed to show up every day." In fact, neither the business nor the mission could exist without the other. They exist in an odd, codependent sort of relationship, often working at cross-purposes. It is not our goal to train the future bean soup makers of America, but we must train the women and run the business as best we can so that we can sell enough product and generate the revenue to hire the women and teach them how to be employees.

Most businesses try to hire the best workers. Women's Bean Project hires the worst, so we can help the neediest women in the community. Women who come to the Bean Project often lack what most adults would consider basic life skills. This includes problem solving; when her child care falls apart, does she have the skills necessary to break down the problem and address it as needed? Communication: can she communicate in an effective way with others, especially during conflict? Goal setting: can she set her sights on improving her life and take the necessary steps toward accomplishing the goal?

At the Bean Project, our policy is three no-calls-no-shows lead to termination. It takes a lot for someone to be fired from the Bean. After all, it is our mission to work with women and help them become productive employees. Most often, women are let go because of attendance. As an incentive, program participants earn paid days off when they maintain 90 percent or better attendance. We are never looking to fire a woman, but we are very clear that coming to work is one of the most important aspects of keeping a job. Across America, absenteeism is one of the top reasons people are fired.

From one day to the next, we rarely know how many women will come to work—another of the challenges in running a business whose workers have so many barriers to employment. Each woman is also allowed up to five hours of paid time off in every two-week pay period to take care of basic needs. Perhaps she has a meeting for affordable housing or with her parole officer. She might have a doctor appointment. Regardless, if she follows the guidelines, she will be paid for those five hours. On top of that are the women who miss work unpredictably for a myriad of reasons. Children are often at the heart of these absences.

Rena's son was taken away from her at birth as she entered prison for driving under the influence. Matter-of-factly, she told me how her husband was beating her while she was driving and how she ran into a retaining wall, seriously injuring a friend who was sitting in the backseat. She described how her husband ran from the car before the police arrived, leaving Rena to be arrested. Her son was four years old when she got out of prison and regained custody. Rena began working at the Bean Project and hired her fourteen-year-old daughter to watch her son. He was displaying behavioral and developmental problems, perhaps related to her drinking while pregnant and exacerbated by their separation so soon after birth. For the first several weeks of her employment, she frequently received phone calls, either from her daughter or from the police, reporting that her son had run away. Despite being in his sister's care, he found ways to escape their apartment and was found wandering the streets. Rena's face became flushed when she told her supervisor that she had to leave work so she could rush home to address the problem, fearing that the police might someday follow up on their promise to turn her son over to Child Protective Services instead of calling her.

Rena was very competent at the Bean Project, but the chaos in her life threatened her job and certainly would have ended her employment with a mainstream employer. We focused on trying to help her get a subsidy so she could afford better child care. Additionally, we referred her to services that provided children with screening and therapy before they enrolled in school.

At Women's Bean Project, every product is assembled by hand, which makes the work labor intensive. All products are assembled from dry ingredients into Bean Project packaging with a tag that says "Lovingly Handmade by" and a handwritten name identifying a woman in the program whose life is being directly affected by the sale of the product. Each necklace, pair of earrings or bracelet is assembled, bead by bead, by the women and packaged with its own Lovingly Handmade tag. This labor intensity presents its own challenges. In some ways it makes sense to keep the work highly manual to create more jobs, but there is a fine line at which labor intensity becomes overly burdensome and unreasonably costly. Yet there is an unrelenting pressure to hire more women. The influx of new applications is constant, and we turn away four out of five women who apply.

Our applicants just want a second chance. They have heard our program works, and they want their opportunity. While we are always trying to grow our businesses so we can hire more women, the more we hire, the more challenging it is to manage a group with poor interpersonal skills. They are not a group who knows how to productively resolve conflict, tactfully state their opinions or brush off a slight.

Some days I wonder how we are able to accomplish anything, but most times it all seems to come together. Product gets made, sold and sent to customers who enjoy the delicious treats. We make enough money to pay our employees and buy more beans to keep the business rolling. Foundations and individual donors believe enough in what we do to give their money and faith, providing the financial support needed to pay the women when they participate in skills training that is essential to their eventual success. Seventy-five percent of our operating budget comes from the sale of our products, and although we would love for this self-supporting portion to increase, I wonder if the inefficiencies in our model make that goal impossible. It is never easy. No woman has only one issue, and often the multiple issues conspire to make it that much harder to create a new life. The program is a metaphor for the business.

Watching program participants blossom before my eyes has been one of the primary benefits of this job. It is all the more rewarding when we are able to hire our own graduates. Graduates are uniquely qualified to understand the challenges facing program participants. They can relate to the barriers that a history of addiction and felony convictions present, and they have a unique credibility. And yet, the program graduates we hire seem to think they need to display superhuman capabilities.

As we approached the 2006 holiday season, we had hired Shaniqua, a recent program graduate, to lead the shipping department. By then, we were receiving orders from several sources, including all the Kroger grocery stores in Colorado, overstock.com and amazon.com. Even our own website sales had grown significantly. We were rocking! But we had no electronic means for processing orders. Each order had to be hand-entered into our accounting system to create a packing slip, then physically walked downstairs and placed into a tray in the shipping department. During the off-season, between March and August, this system wasn't an issue. During that period, we could handle it all manually. Seventy percent of our sales are made between October and January, though, and this manual system wasn't scalable. To give some idea of the volume: on any given day in July or August of 2006, there were perhaps twenty packages that required picking, packing and shipping. During that year's holiday season we received between 200 and 600 orders every day. By assigning Shaniqua to focus on order fulfillment we believed we had it under control. And we did—for a while.

Shaniqua was grateful to have so much faith placed in her. As a program participant she had come out of her shell. Her inability to look me in the eye on her first day of work confirmed what she reported: she had no self-esteem. When she came to the Bean Project, she was heavy, having gained fifty pounds in prison because of her schizophrenia medication. She hid her body in long-sleeved t-shirts and grungy overalls. Though she hated this side effect, she recognized that the medication kept her mentally stable, a program requirement.

Boy, was she a hard worker. Surprisingly so, once she shared her story. She had been raised by her grandmother after her mother left. Her father was an addict and already gone by the time she was old enough to be aware that she had a father. Despite her lack of strong role models, she took great pride in how much work she could do without help.

Shaniqua had taken a long and arduous path to the Bean Project. At twelve, she began acting out, and her grandmother placed her in the first of many group homes until she and a friend ran away. This situation ended when the friend stabbed Shaniqua during a disagreement, leading Shaniqua to live on the streets. At fourteen, she had her first baby. To support the child, she sold crack. Surprisingly, she stayed in school until she was sixteen and gave birth to her second child. She overcame many obstacles and became a Certified Nursing Assistant when she was eighteen.

In the intervening five years or so, Shaniqua entered and left an abusive relationship and married and divorced a sex offender. Finally, she was arrested for selling crack when she was twenty-two and sentenced to probation. She'd been involved only in drug sales up until that point but finally transitioned to using crack when she was twenty-three and started "hooking" to support her addiction. This lifestyle did not last long; she was convicted of prostitution and possession, and served two and a half years in prison.

When we decided to invite Shaniqua to continue working at the Bean Project as team leader in the shipping department through the holiday season, we discussed her dual role of shipping and role model for the other women. "That won't be a problem," she said, flashing the quick smile I knew so well. "The support you all give helps me keep going and wanting to stay straight. I've learned how to be a reliable employee. You gave me a chance to show who I really am. Instead of looking at the negative things about me, everyone here looks at the positive things. I've finally quit beating myself up."

We were set, then. Shaniqua would oversee getting all the packages out the door. As team leader of the shipping department, she would have the perfect opportunity to be a role model to the other women. Even before the holiday season began, Shaniqua came to work each morning at 7 a.m. She wasn't required to be at work until eight, but she took advantage of an earlier bus to arrive early and begin working.

During the holiday season, I often act as a floater; taking on whatever job in whichever department I am needed. I noted that the shipping department was getting busier and inventory was getting lower. Shaniqua began staying at work later and later. Every day for a week we replayed a scene in which I offered her help and she said she had it under control. I talked with her supervisor and he didn't want to interfere, trusting that if she said she was fine, she was.

Yet, I could see the pile of orders grow taller and taller, until it was nearly four inches high; each sheet represented an order, someone counting on us to send their special gift to arrive by Christmas. The pile of orders grew daily while I watched and fretted, offering help and being turned down.

Finally, Geoff, our sales director, pulled me aside. "I think you should know that Shaniqua is staying late every night." I acknowledged that I knew. But he clarified: "No, she is clocking out and continuing to stay—sometimes until 2 a.m.!" He was concerned about the orders, but also about Shaniqua's well-being. I resolved to act. I could no longer sit on the sidelines and watch her flounder.

On the morning of December 1, I dressed in jeans and a sweatshirt, casual clothes that would make it easy for me to stand all day and work in the shipping department. I arrived at 8 a.m., hung my purse and coat in my upstairs office and walked down to the shipping department. Shaniqua already was hard at work. I approached her with a smile and asked again what I could do, expecting to be told "nothing." Except this time I had decided I was not going to accept nothing for an answer.

"It's clear you are overwhelmed, but we have the resources to help you. You can tell me what you would like me to do, or I will start doing what I think should be done," I told Shaniqua in a friendly, but firm voice.

She turned away, toward the computer screen, and refused to answer. To her back I said, "I'm sorry that you are not willing to accept my help, but I'm not giving you a choice. Getting these orders out the door has to take priority. Our customers are counting on us to get their gifts to their family and friends. I know you don't want to let them down." Again, silence.

I picked up the pile of orders and started reviewing them, trying to discern what kind of system Shaniqua was using to prioritize which orders would be shipped and when. When it was not immediately apparent, I asked, "How are these organized? Where would you like me to start?" I was determined not to belittle her. My goal was to help, not hinder.

Without answering, Shaniqua stood up, walked the twenty feet from the shipping department to the production floor and inserted herself into the bean soup line in progress. I stood for a moment in disbelief. What was she doing? Was she choosing to leave her assigned job in her refusal to accept help?

I decided to assess the situation before I acted. Once again, I began looking through the pile of orders. There did not appear to be a system for the pile, except chronological. As I began to get closer to the bottom of the pile, I discovered orders two and three weeks old. Unable to discern why some orders had been sent and others not, I decided to approach Shaniqua at the production line and ask about the orders, how she had prioritized them and why some of the older ones had not been sent.

She wouldn't assist. That was Shaniqua's last day working in the shipping department, and shortly afterward she quit. By the end of the season our sales had grown forty percent. We hadn't anticipated that kind of growth. Without meaning to, we had set her up for failure. There was no way for her to succeed, but she would have rather died trying than admit she needed help.

We do this to some graduates. They become so successful in our safe place that we glom onto them and their success, creating expectations and responsibilities. The women respond in a variety of ways. Some of them self-sabotage. I think I understand why; it is the converse of my own personal demons. Fear of failure has motivated me to do many things that I might not otherwise have had the wherewithal to pursue, finish or even start. But if failure is all you are used to, success is very scary. Fulfilling the expectation of failure is safe. Imagine going to work every day, lining up a pistol toward your foot, and shooting. That sort of self-sabotage feels like what we do every day. I approached the job thinking I had a lot to learn but believed those things were related to understanding how to run the business. I had no concept of what it took to operate a manufacturing operation while changing lives. How does one motivate a workforce with a history of chronic unemployment, a group who quits rather than stays to resolve issues? What are the keys to balancing the business demands and the needs of clients struggling to gain stability? I have learned much about managing an organization that is a strange marriage between business and mission. I've never been entirely certain we are doing everything correctly, but I know we'll continue to make improvements until we figure it out. We have to. The women and all those who will come after them are counting on it.

CHAPTER 2

CULTURE CLASH—
HOW I LEARNED TO STEP BEYOND MY
SUBURBAN, MIDDLE-CLASS ROOTS

Sharon was one of the first women I met at the Bean Project and she's emblematic of how different I felt from the program participants. She was a tall, dark-skinned African American woman who intimidated me when we met. She came across as angry, but I guessed she was guarded because of her experiences with the criminal justice system and with authority in general. She rarely smiled and didn't look me in the eye when we spoke. Her scowl made her seem scary, but sometimes, when she didn't know I was looking, I saw her face soften and sensed some sensitivity and warmth beneath the icy façade.

Sharon came to work every day, on time, and stayed on task. We used a heat sealer for the spice packages, a one-person job that entailed sitting on a chair in front of the sealer, placing each three-by-four-inch bag on the base, stepping on the pedal that lowered the heating element, and holding it for just the right amount of time to seal the bag but not melt off the end. Sharon was great at it. The heat sealer was located next to a brick pillar close to an electrical outlet. That placed it out of the way and off to side of the production line, isolating whoever was assigned the task. Though not necessary, Sharon chose to sit in the task chair next to the heat sealer with her back to the room for extended periods, in her own world, hardly speaking to anyone.

I knew from her case file that Sharon had struggled for many years with addiction and mental illness, relapsing and going back to prison several times. Her crimes usually involved drug possession, but she also sold drugs and a few times resorted to prostitution to support her habit. When we met, she had several adult children, one with mental illness more severe than Sharon's and on her way to an equally complicated life as an addict and felon.

At the time, I didn't know what it meant to be institutionalized, but I learned later that Sharon's behavior demonstrated just that. She sat with her back to the room because she didn't want to interact or deal with reality. Later, another program participant explained that she had seen women in prison who'd go to the gym with fellow inmates, but isolate themselves in a corner, with their backs to the room, bouncing a ball by themselves. Being institutionalized means that an individual is better able to cope inside the walls of prison where there is structure and options are severely limited. After many years of being told what to do, some inmates lose the ability to think for themselves. Transitioning from the highly structured environment of prison or halfway houses—or even rehab—into the community, where there are seemingly unlimited choices, can be overwhelming. As a result, many people, consciously or not, self-sabotage in order to go back to the structure. Essentially, they are more comfortable in an institution. I'd often hear program participants refer to someone who'd gone back to prison as being institutionalized. It always sounded as though it was a combination of a judgment for not being able to make it and sadness that they couldn't.

Every culture has its own set of rules. We can be hard-pressed to identify or explain these rules. They just are. The women's cultures, whether the drug culture, the prison culture, or street culture, were as unfamiliar to me as any language in a foreign country. Part of my education at the Bean Project was getting a glimpse into these cultures and allowing the women to teach me. As with any education, there was a cost, but in my case, the price I paid was often my pride. By being willing to ask questions and risk embarrassment, I gained insight into the women's worlds.

Early in my tenure I didn't understand the dynamic my position created. I was anxious to get to know the women, mainly because I desperately wanted to understand what motivated them. If I could understand that, I thought I could help drive productivity. There also was a part of me that wanted to be liked. I'd never been surrounded by so many people with whom I had so little in common, and I hoped I could find some common ground. I saw Sharon as a special challenge because she was difficult to get to know. I frequently focused my attention on her, trying to get her to open up. One day, about an hour after lunch, I walked past Sharon, who was sitting, just as she had that morning, at the heat sealer. I'd had a casual conversation with her earlier, so this time, on impulse, I walked up behind her and rubbed her left shoulder a bit, "Sharon, are you getting tired from sitting here for so long today? Would you like to trade jobs...?" Before I could finish, she jumped up and turned on me defensively.

"That don't fly!" She said something else that I didn't catch. I felt the room get smaller, the radio suddenly seeming louder. I didn't look around, but I could feel the other women on the production floor watching to see what would happen next.

"I didn't mean to startle you. I'm sorry." I tried to engage her in eye contact, hoping I could convince her I meant no harm, but she was looking at the ground.

"Don't touch me like that! Don't come up behind me and touch me!"

Her reaction wasn't that of being startled. It was defensiveness out of proportion to the situation—or at least the way I intended my touch. She seemed prepared to fight, leaning away from me, shoulders tight, fists clenched. It was precisely the opposite of what I'd intended. I often use light touch, either on the forearm or the shoulder, to build rapport. My touches had never before been mistaken as aggressive. I'd also never had difficulty getting to know people and moving beyond their defenses. Some new relationships might require a little extra effort, but I nearly always worked through the initial discomfort. I was about to learn, for the first of many times, that my past experience didn't come close to preparing me for the culture at the Bean Project.

Later I asked Maude, the production supervisor who had witnessed the situation, what else Sharon had said to me when she jumped. "Oh, she said 'don't put the timi on me,'" she replied matter-of-factly.

I'm sure Sharon didn't really think about her response before she gave it. If she had, she'd have realized I wouldn't understand her. The "timi"—she was accusing me of intimidation. Maude explained that Sharon thought I was making a sexual overture. Later I learned that lesbian relationships are often part of the subculture, and sex is used for power in prison. Lesbian relationships can emerge for a variety of reasons. Some women are gay when they go to prison and develop relationships while there. Others develop relationships, both sexual and nonsexual, as a result of their isolation from loved ones. Because women often relate through touch, it follows that intimate relationships could develop while locked up. Some women are straight when they are out of prison, but gay while they are in. It was a long time before I knew enough women well enough to ask questions about these dynamics. That day, not for the last time, I had stepped into a situation that involved cultural cues I couldn't read and an unfamiliar dynamic.

I tried to find a way to redeem the relationship. A few days later, as the afternoon's work was ending, the program participants had finished cleaning the equipment on the production floor and were preparing labels and name tags for the next day. The last thirty minutes of the day often concluded this way, with the women sitting around the production tables, chatting and doing these easy tasks. It always reminds me of a knitting circle or a quilting bee. As I walked by the group I heard Sharon say, "I gotta go drop."

I assumed she meant drop someone off. I thought Sharon took the bus to work, so dropping someone off seemed complicated and I wondered if she would even be allowed to, since she lived in a halfway house. My curiosity got the best of me and I insinuated myself into the conversation, "Who are you dropping off, Sharon?"

She looked at me like I was crazy. "Dropping off?" she asked flatly.

"Yeah, I heard you say you had to go drop. Did you mean drop off a person?" I could already tell by the smiles on the other women's faces that I was mistaken.

"Drop a U/A."

I was about to learn an important lesson: when you are a well-educated white girl in a group of street-wise women of color, there is a lot you don't know. The least I could do was give them the opportunity to teach me something. I could cede power and begin my street education. I already felt like an idiot, so I figured I had nothing to lose. I smiled, "You know I am going to ask this because I'm a dumb white girl. What's a U-A?"

Referring to myself as a dumb white girl lifted the tension. All of the women began to pitch in with a quick tutorial on urinalysis, U/A for short. Nearly all of them were monitored in some way, either as a part of their term at a halfway house or as a condition of their parole. They taught me about "hot" U/As, when the urine tests come back from the lab showing a positive result for illegal substances. I learned that the temperature of the urine is checked when a sample is dropped, to make sure it wasn't provided by someone else and carried in a container to the facility. A urine sample that isn't body temperature is a giveaway that the subject has something to hide and has brought someone else's urine for testing. It is automatically counted as hot, and a hot U/A can send a woman back to prison.

I learned even more about U/As when we began doing drug tests as a condition of hire. We contracted with a clinic to come to the Bean Project and take all of the samples at one sitting. The clinic sends a nurse, and we round up all of the program participants and seat them in the conference room while, one by one, they go into the attached restroom and provide a sample. Each time at least one woman starts by saying that she is really dehydrated and not able to give a sample. "I can't pee," she'll insist. The nurse gives her glass after glass of water and requires the woman to drink each glass in her presence. The program participant isn't allowed to leave the room until she gives a sample. Or, a woman suddenly says she's feeling ill and needs to leave for the day. These behaviors are harbingers of hot U/As.

After the samples are sent to the lab, negative results—clean tests—come back to us right away. We always breathe a sigh of relief for those women, knowing they can stay in the program. But there always are one or two samples in each group that have to be "sent to the lab." Sent to the lab means the U/A is dirty with some substance and further testing is required to determine exactly what is in it. Until the detailed test results come back, even the clinic physician doesn't know what will found in the sample, so he calls each woman to ask if she is taking any prescription medications, such as psychotropic drugs, that might make the sample hot.

It is usually at this point that a woman will approach a staff member and say, "OK, I did smoke pot a few weeks ago, but I haven't had any lately." Or "I was in the room when other people were smoking crack. I didn't use, but it might have gotten in my system." Regardless of the reason, a hot U/A means immediate termination.

One woman pulled Luanne, our HR manager and controller, aside to explain why her test came back positive for cocaine. She sat down in the chair next to Luanne's desk, looked over her shoulder to ensure the coast was clear, and confessed, "I don't use, but I have been selling crack. So that might be why my test is positive." Luanne thanked her for her honesty and provided her last paycheck.

Drug testing was only the beginning of my education. I also learned that crack is "rock," and meth is "crank" or "dope" or "crystal." Besides dropping a U/A, "drop" also can mean dropping off drugs. Getting "shit" means going to get drugs. The original methamphetamine twenty years ago didn't ruin people's teeth the way today's meth does. The chemicals used to manufacture the more recent meth ruins teeth and creates blackened stumps in the mouths of many women I meet. I began to pay closer attention to women's mouths. When a former meth addict's teeth appear healthy and white, my first question is always "What about your teeth?" She'll often show me the corrosion in other parts of her mouth. I spend a lot of time looking at other people's teeth.

Heroin has many names, including "junk," "smack," and "cheese." If someone disappears for the weekend to get high on "H," she "got all cheesed out." Crammers are people who shoot up. When coming off a high or getting clean, one is "kickin'" it. Whether accurately or not, the women believe that kickin' it from heroin is much worse than meth.

Mary and Brianna were sitting at one of the computer stations where program participants practice typing and learn other essential computer skills. I sat next to them and asked about some expressions about meth use that I'd heard but didn't understand. Both women had ruined their teeth with meth. They smiled at each other as I asked each question, as though they were letting me in on trade secrets. Cringing, they described the horrors of heroin withdrawal. "One girl I saw in jail thought she had bugs crawling on her," Brianna said with a shudder. Fear of the heroin withdrawal kept both of them loyal to meth.

As my understanding of the vernacular grew, so did my awareness of my surroundings. I began to understand there was a parallel world going on around me about which I had only a dawning knowledge. One sunny weekday afternoon, I was running errands during my lunch hour and drove into the parking lot of a convenience store intending to buy a Diet Coke. As I turned off my car I noticed a scrawny, unkempt white guy sitting on the curb at the side of the building. It crossed my mind that perhaps he was resting or enjoying the sun, but something didn't fit. As I sat watching him, a tall black guy strutted up. His hoodie, jeans and sneakers made him appear overdressed for the heat of the day. The white guy stood to greet the black guy; they did a fist-bump-handshake, said a couple of words and then walked away in opposite directions. It took me a moment to digest what I'd seen. I realized I'd just seen a drug exchange. I didn't know who was the seller and who the purchaser; it all happened too slyly and quickly. My street education had forever shifted my view of the world.

No longer do I look at two sneakers tied together and hung over a telephone wire as an innocent prank. It means drugs can be purchased at that location. I wonder how many dozens of pairs of sneakers hanging on telephone wires I'd missed because I never knew to look. For a long time, there were sneakers hanging outside my office window. Once I knew their significance, I paid closer attention to the park across the street and noticed frequent, brief interactions between people. One person will be waiting in the park. Another person will walk up. They appear to talk for a moment and then part. I see the world through a different lens and realize how much I was missing because these events weren't within my social realm. I think about how this same concept applies to the women. If they have no reference points for employment or other social experiences that are normal in my world, they are just as naive as I about how to conduct themselves. Just because my experiences are considered mainstream is no reason to assume they could automatically act appropriately without the same kind of assistance I was receiving from them.

The women took my education seriously, wanting to ensure I knew the important facts and expressions. If I was going to learn, then I should really learn. One program graduate offered to take me to the Triangle, the area downtown near the homeless shelter where the unemployed addicts hung out during the day. If I wanted to talk to someone who could tell me about recent drug experiences, she could arrange it. I was content to hear it from the program participants. They wanted me to know things like the importance of never getting "wooed," which meant someone had sold you bad drugs or had just taken your money. "You done got wooed." That is bad. Even worse is a "dirt nap." That means someone is killed and left on the ground. I once overheard the following conversation between two women, "That man they found down the street? He was takin' a dirt nap."

"Ooo, girl. There ain't no coming back from that."

Someone doesn't get convicted of a crime, they "catch a case." Or they "done caught a case," when telling another. As a result, they "gotta go to court."

When someone gets sentenced, I'd hear they "got a five bit" or a "ten piece." A five bit with a two-year tail means she received a five-year sentence with two-years of parole. Because of prison overcrowding, Colorado is a mandatory parole state, meaning everyone who goes to prison also ends up on parole. An inmate automatically starts with the assumption she will serve just half of her sentence. Additional time off is available for good behavior, although the minimum time served is about 38 percent. When it is time to go off to prison, you are "puttin' your bid in" or "doing your time." If you get in trouble while in prison, the punishment may be solitary confinement in a twenty-three-hour lockdown, "the hole" or "the shoe." "Got sent back" is a return to prison, which can happen for a variety of reasons.

Once out of prison and at the halfway house, or the "way-way," one can still get lockdowns, but not as often as while in prison. In a halfway house no one wants to be "hot." That isn't a compliment on their appearance, it means the halfway house staff is suspicious of the resident's activities and is keeping a close eye on her. Maybe they think she is using again, or associating with someone she isn't supposed to, or bringing contraband into the halfway house.

Aurelia came in to work one day frustrated because she wanted to start taking evening community college classes while she was still living in the halfway house. They had told her no, college is a privilege, not a right. Aurelia's disappointed response to me was, "Way-way won't let a girl come up."

The women taught me that no matter how much time has passed, it's a minute. During one of my visits to the grocery store in the neighborhood, I stood in the checkout line between two black women from the neighborhood who greeted one another as though they hadn't seen each other for some time. They each asked after several people, finally getting to a guy named Royshawn, whom it was clear they both knew.

"Yeah, he was in prison for a minute, but he out now," the woman in front of me said.

"Oh, good," the other woman replied, unfazed. "Tell his mama I said hey."

One afternoon near the end of a busy week, Bob, our director of services, and I were talking about the group of women we employed at the time, discussing their backgrounds and who'd been to prison. It led to a discussion of the various euphemisms for jail and prison. Though at the time I don't think I knew the difference between jail and prison, I knew a lot of names for the institutions. The "pokey," "gray bar hotel," "the slammer," "the clink," "the big house." In New York, I'd heard "He's gone upstate." The "house of numbers" referred to the fact that prison inmates didn't have names, they had numbers.

I don't recall where I learned all of these expressions, but I never heard a program participant use any of them. They were slang terms that were a part of my vernacular, but they didn't seem to be used by the women I met who had actually gone to jail and prison. The women I met stated without hesitation that they'd been into prison or jail. There was no beating around the bush. Perhaps the closest I heard to a euphemism from the program participants was "I was locked up." Locked up is essentially an umbrella term for not having one's freedom, but it isn't a way to soften the reference to incarceration. Other expressions I learned related to the criminal justice system revolved around the Department of Corrections (DOC). Prisoners are not routinely referred to by name; one's DOC number is one's identity until a felon is "off paper," or off parole. One of the most rewarding experiences I have at the Bean is when a woman shares with me a letter from the Board of Parole that "kills her number." This letter tells the world that she has finally fulfilled the requirements of her sentence. The letters I see are simple, white sheets of paper with her name and DOC number at the top, followed by a few short paragraphs saying that she's complied with all of the requirements of the law and is discharged from her sentence, with an effective date.

The first time I saw one of these letters was when Lorraine showed me hers. Her light brown skin was flushed when she walked in the front door of the Bean Project. I was happy to see her; she'd graduated a couple of months earlier and continued to stop by frequently. I could see in her smile that this day was different. She nearly skipped as she approached me, handing me a white sheet of paper with a mysterious smile. Knowing that her look was my prompt to read the paper, but not knowing what it was, I was surprised by its simplicity, given the impact it would have on Lorraine's life. No more random drug tests or missing work to visit her "PO," parole officer. Though she'd always have a felony record, she now was free to put her life back together.

"What do you do with this now?" I asked, assuming it would get filed away, but would never be needed.

"Oh, I'll carry it with me for a while," Lorraine said earnestly.

"Why would you need to have it with you? Don't you want to keep it in a file—somewhere safe?"

"If I were to get stopped, the police would ask me if I was on parole. If I said no, but the system said I was still on, they'd pick me up." Apparently it was common knowledge that there is a lag between the discharge letter being sent and the rest of the system catching up. I knew, for Lorraine's sake, it wasn't worth the risk.

The women always act respectfully toward me, though initially the respect is guarded, like what they are required to show halfway house staff members or any of the myriad of people with power over their futures. Eventually we become well enough acquainted that they share their discharge letters as Lorraine had. Some even ask me to write recommendation letters for them when they go to the Parole Board. With each group of women, I eventually build enough trust that I can ask questions about the slang they use. Each time I ask, the conversation dynamic shifts. I become the pupil, they are the teachers. I can see they enjoy it. Rather than invading, I am showing respect for their culture and building relationships with them simply by asking questions. After hearing each expression, I try it out, and the women always laugh, partly embarrassed for me, but also because of the disconnect of hearing their expressions come out of my mouth. "You don't sound ghetto enough," they'll say. My "Yo, yo, what up?" or "Hey, girl!" greeting in the morning never quite sounds right and always elicits giggles from the women.

I'm not able to put to use everything I learn. For instance, I've never found an opportunity to refer to the police as the "Poe-lees," accent on the Poe. Anyone in a position of authority is referred to as the poe-lees as well as several other expressions, like "Po-po," "Five-O," and "Rollers." Someone with less authority, say, a security person on public transportation, is called "Deputy No-badge" or a "cop with a flashlight."

I learned not to say, "He picked her up in a stolen car." It's a G-ride for reasons no one can explain. However, a G-Ride can also be a gangster car. If someone refers to a guy as a "G," that means he's a gangster and is likely to drive a Cutlass or a Cadillac, unless of course, he has moved into a Big Body—a truck—the prevailing trend for a G's car choice.

Someone isn't on welfare, it's "assistance." It is acceptable to be on assistance, but not acceptable to be a "welfare mom." That means she isn't doing what she is supposed to be doing, taking care of her kids and looking for a job to move her life forward. Instead, it means she is using and "hooking," or prostituting, to support her drug habit. She might be living with her "john," the guy who manages her prostitution for a cut of the proceeds. The john might also be her drug supplier and even her "baby daddy."

A man is not the father of a child, he is the baby daddy. Baby daddies don't stay around to be a part of the family. One guy might be the baby daddy for several women who may even know each other.

I have entire conversations that would have never occurred to me before I began working at the Bean Project. One day I wanted to take a picture of Jessie because we were featuring her quote in our catalog. I asked if she would take a break from the jewelry production because I needed to get her picture. Jessie looked much older than her thirty-four years because all her teeth were missing. She lacked the facial structure teeth provided, so sometimes, to be silly, she'd scrunch up her face like an apple that had been carved and allowed to dry up, creating the look of a voodoo-shrunken head. Even with just her top dentures in, she appeared dozens of years younger than without them. When I approached her, camera in hand, to take her picture, she said, "Sure, but can we wait until tomorrow? I want to bring my teeth."

"Well, there you go. I never get to say that. I always have my teeth with me. I don't even have the option of leaving them at home." Jessie smiled her toothless grin in reply.

Jessie had left her top dentures at home because the bottom set didn't fit. Though hard for me to imagine, it was more comfortable to go without teeth than to wear dentures that didn't fit properly.

Fortunately, in all my time at the Bean Project, no one has ever said to me, "Why you actin' all brand new?" This means acting as though you don't know something that you should. When I first started working at the Bean Project I was mostly concerned about my appearance and not standing out too much. I thought about whether or not I should wear my diamond engagement ring or get a different car—at the time I drove a BMW sedan. I realize these are outward expressions of my socioeconomic status, but it isn't as though I'd be fooling anyone if I changed my appearance, accessories or mode of transportation. I can't hide my education or the fact that I'm white. Instead I'd risk being accused of the serious offense of "fakin' to fit in." This would be worse than merely not fitting in.

My position as CEO puts me at a different level than the women. I am referred to as "the director," which, in their world, means the person in charge. The fact that I sign their paychecks is evidence enough of our differences. I decided that it was more important for me to be authentic. Hiding aspects of my life would be an affront. I need to be approachable. I want to be. I want to learn. By being my true, naive self, I give them the opportunity to teach me, laugh at me and hopefully even bond with me.

Occasionally, after I get to know a group of women enough, I'll ask what they thought of me when they first started working at Women's Bean Project. I wonder if their opinion changes once we become acquainted. It is probably dumb to ask. Who is going to say something bad about the person who signs their paychecks or who has the power to fire them?

Despite the various outward expressions of culture—theirs and mine—I had to get past the divisions our positions fostered if I was ever going to learn. I, the middle-class CEO of the organization and they, the impoverished, recovering addicts and felons of the program. What could we possibly have in common? Ultimately, my curiosity and willingness to ask questions have brought us closer.

While it is a bit of a game we play, I think we all enjoy it. I am sincerely interested in understanding the women, their pressures, their worlds. It is amusing to learn expressions I have no other reason to know. With the women in the safe haven of the Bean, I can try on these personas, if only for a few moments at a time. But my willingness to learn helps create long-lasting bridges.

CHAPTER 3

TWO STEPS FORWARD, THREE STEPS BACK— HOW POVERTY SELF-PERPETUATES

For the first time in her life, Janine seemed to be doing everything right. The year prior to being hired at Women's Bean Project, when she was thirty-four, she earned her GED. Then she enrolled in college. Her dream was to open a facility for transitional housing, a place for people like her—at least, like she used to be. At the Bean she was reliable, with remarkable attention to detail and a great attitude. Though not married, she wore a ring on her left hand so "no one bothered her." I suspect her concern was legitimate. She had a bright smile and beautifully arched eyebrows. By all accounts, Janine was doing all she could to support her four children and push them to graduate from high school and go to college. It was hard to watch Janine try so hard while witnessing how the human services system worked against her. But I was to learn that Janine's experience wasn't unique.

I asked Janine if I could talk to her about her background. When she gave me the okay, we scheduled a time, near the end of the day, when the shipping department wasn't busy. We sat in one corner of the shipping area, in chairs we'd taken from nearby desks. She smiled at me, eagerly waiting for the questions. I asked if she would talk about what it was like to grow up in a poor family, but I wasn't expecting the story I heard.

"Was your family poor when you were growing up?"

"Oh yes, I am the youngest child and only daughter of two drug-addicted parents."

"Were there role models for employment around you as a child?"

"I didn't know anyone who worked."

Surely there was someone? An aunt or cousin?

She shook her head.

"But who took care of you when you were little?"

"Sometimes my Grammy took care of me, but I always wanted to go home and make sure my mom was okay. I thought I needed to take care of her." Her earnestness struck me. She was very matter of fact, continuing to look me in the eye, still smiling occasionally. She harbored no ill feelings, these were just the facts. Not good or bad, just the way it was.

"How did you eat?"

"My mom got assistance. She went down to the office and got the food stamps."

I asked if these experiences made her feel different from her peers.

"I was embarrassed because I didn't have clothes. My Grammy and my aunts would buy me clothes—for my birthday and Christmas—so I would have something to wear to school."

"So, when you went home to be with your mother, who took care of you?"

"I took care of myself, but I always felt unsafe." She went on to explain that things began to change when she was twelve and she started selling crack, making enough money to get her own apartment.

"Wait, you were twelve? Who signed the lease?"

"My mom. I was her supplier. She wanted to support me. I used to sell to my mom, my dad, their friends...." Her voice trailed off, and for the first time, she looked away.

"Did you ever use crack?" I asked, to pull Janine back to the conversation.

She nodded. "I started using when I was sixteen. I sold to be closer to my mom. When that didn't work, I started using with my mom." Her revised strategies also didn't work, and eventually Janine became pregnant and dropped out of school in the eleventh grade. Although she stopped using, she continued to sell crack on her own to support herself and her son. Through the births of three more children, she continued, until eventually she became caught up with big-time drug dealers. She thought she had it made — financially speaking. Finally, she was convicted on federal charges for possession with intent to distribute and sentenced to fifty-four months in federal prison. She left her kids — by then four of them — and spent several years in the women's federal penitentiary.

What happened to her kids during that time, I wondered aloud.

"By the time I went to prison, my mom was clean, so she took care of them."

But Janine realized the impact her absence had on her kids. After her release she worked daily to set an example and lead them down a different path than the one she'd taken. Despite her ardent desire and laser focus on creating a new life, Janine still had a lot working against her. When I met her, she owed over $15,000 in back child support. As her employer, we were ordered to garnish half of her paycheck. I wanted to know more about her kids and when I asked, she lit up, smiling and leaning forward in her chair, excited to tell me about them.

"I have four kids. My oldest boy is a senior in high school. He plays football. My second one is thirteen. She plays basketball."

"They must eat a lot?"

Janine smiled broadly, "They do! I get $150 a month in food stamps."

"You feed all four kids with $150 a month? How is that possible?"

"It's not easy, but I make it work." Proudly Janine described how she went to the meat market and bought a fifty-dollar meat pack to last the month. She was an avid coupon user and shopped at Sam's Club for bulk items.

These strategies were unfamiliar to me. While I know there were times when my parents struggled to support four children, especially when my dad, a union pipefitter, had been laid off and was waiting for the next job, I had no idea how my experience compared to others. I hadn't had a lot, but I'd always had enough. When I needed shoes, I got them, even if I had only one pair at a time. We always had food, but I suspect my mom was good at creating economical meals. I always got new clothes for school—after we paid off the lay-away. We went on annual two-week vacations, road-trips across the country. I suppose I knew that others had more than my family, but it never occurred to me that others—at least others in America—might have less.

When I became an adult, my worldview became bigger through travel, and I became increasingly aware of poverty. Through my personal and professional travels, I witnessed international poverty, sometimes on a scale that was hard to fathom, even seeing it firsthand. But back at home, it was easy for me to believe that the poor created poverty for themselves. I was moving my way up the socioeconomic ladder. By going to college and then graduate school, I was working to ensure that my life would be better than my parents'. And the truth was, I had never met any poor people in America. They were the people who lived in other parts of the cities. I believed that if you set your mind to it, you could change your life. I had never seen how poverty perpetuates itself and had no perspective on whether or not it was difficult to rise above.

I wonder how many Americans understand what poverty in our country is. Many people are familiar with the international poverty reference point of living on less than a dollar a day. This dollar-a-day income threshold represents absolute poverty, or an income considered to be the absolute minimum to have a decent life.

But a dollar a day is so little by American standards that it can seem as though no one could possibly live in absolute poverty. That's where relative poverty comes in. Relative poverty is defined as living well below a percentage of the national median income. It describes relative deprivation and therefore is more a measure of inequality. In the United States, one typically doesn't hear reference to living on less than a dollar a day, but one does hear about the federal poverty level, which, updated in 2012, set the income level for a family of four at just over $23,000 per year. Every woman we hire at the Bean Project, by virtue of being chronically unemployed, lives below the federal poverty level.

Through my interactions with the women hired at the Bean Project, I began to witness American poverty. Curiously, I saw a simultaneous increase in attention focused on international poverty. While I was personally observing the inescapable challenges impoverished women in my own community faced and how little attention these issues were receiving, I noted the proliferation of organizations formed to address international poverty. It is hard not to be appalled by the unspeakable horrors that women and girls around the world face, victimized by societies that marginalize them to the point of nonexistence. When wealthy Americans think of poverty, what comes to mind is poor women in developing countries without economic opportunity, rights, or even access to fresh water. But I was appalled at how people like me—white, middle-class, educated Americans—were more sympathetic to poverty halfway around the world than poverty down the street. Perhaps in America we are such a pull-yourself-up-by-your-bootstraps culture that we have become intolerant. Intolerant of those we perceive as not trying to change. Intolerant of those we believe milk the system rather than contribute to the base. Intolerant of people who don't follow the rules of getting an education, getting a job and getting married.

What makes people poor isn't just a lack of income. It is also the lack of access to food, housing, health care and basic human rights. And this happens in America too. There are so many factors that get in the way of breaking the cycle of poverty and chronic unemployment. The women we see at the Bean Project fit the mold: they face multiple personal and economic barriers to self-reliance. Our program participants lack marketable skills and stable work histories. Most are single mothers, have histories of public assistance and lack a high school diploma or GED, and many are homeless or at risk of homelessness. Most have histories of incarceration, substance abuse and domestic violence. Women with these backgrounds face enormous challenges to finding and retaining the meaningful employment that is so necessary to break out of poverty. Once in poverty, women face more obstacles than men, such as child care, that trap them. As a result, America has a greater poverty gap between men and women than any other country in the Western World.

Poverty is insidious, like an underwater monster that pulls generation after generation beneath the surface, giving the individuals enough time to take a breath, but not long enough to learn to swim and reach shore. I didn't realize this. I thought people lived in poverty because they were lazy or unmotivated or afraid to make the changes needed to get out.

According to the Brookings Institute, a nonprofit, public policy organization, there are three keys to breaking out of poverty in America: attaining at least a high school education, avoiding single parenthood and maintaining full-time employment. Sounds simple, doesn't it? Only three things; it shouldn't be that hard. Certainly anything is possible in America. Therefore, the only people who aren't breaking out must be causing their own poverty. They lack the will or must have done something—or didn't do the things they were supposed to—to create their problems. This is what I thought, before I met the women at the Bean Project.

A few years before I began working at Women's Bean Project, I became a partner in Social Venture Partners (SVP). I found SVP appealing because it applied a venture capital model to philanthropy, pooling the partners' money and disbursing larger grants to have greater impact on small nonprofit organizations. Monetary contributions are paired with volunteerism, so I signed up for a GED tutoring program we had funded for inner city young adults at the Spot, an evening drop-in center designed to keep kids off of the streets. The kids we tutored already had dropped out of school without getting a high school diploma and were working to get their graduate equivalency degree (GED). Every Wednesday night I went with my husband to the Spot and helped prepare these youth for the GED tests. As I sat with them one-on-one, I learned that many had gotten lost academically around the third grade. Even though many of them had advanced through school, I imagined their growing despair as they fell further and further behind with each grade.

One evening I was helping a girl prepare for the civics portion of the GED test she would take the following day. We were sitting at an eight-foot table in two folding chairs. Fluorescent lights overhead hummed and supplied a yellow cast onto us. Though from her face she appeared to be about eighteen, the way she sat slumped next to me at the table, barely interested in the work we were doing, made her seem younger. She had chosen to come for tutoring that evening, and I figured she really did want to be there, even if she didn't want to appear eager. We arrived at a question that described a scenario in which a group was holding a peaceful march to bring awareness to a cause in which they believed. The question asked which amendment to the U.S. Constitution protected the group's right to have a march. Not only did she have no idea that the answer was the First Amendment, she had no concept of what the Bill of Rights was. I watched as she became increasingly agitated, her, jean-clad knee bouncing with increasing speed. I wanted to resolve the problem quickly, before I lost her, but I had never tried to explain free speech, one of the basic tenets of our country, to another American adult. However, her educational base was not that of a grown-up. Her fund of knowledge about things that I considered basic was entirely lacking. That was the first time I realized how I took for granted everything I had learned throughout my education and life experiences. The love of reading that my parents had encouraged by buying me books and providing opportunities for me to retreat into them was their greatest gift and it set me up for future success.

The odds were against this young woman unless she completed her GED. Those who drop out of school are three and a half times more likely than graduates to be incarcerated, and they have a disproportionately higher unemployment rate. Dropouts cost America in lost wages, lost taxes and lost productivity. Fast forward fifteen or more years, and she could be one of the women who are hired by the Bean Project. More than half of the women who work at Women's Bean Project have neither a diploma nor a GED and have suffered the consequences. Many drop out of school when they have their first child. Some are close to graduating when they stop going to school. We encourage these women to work toward their GED while they are in the program. If a program participant is committed to getting her GED, we pay her during the time she takes a preparation course. In other instances, there is just too large a gap to fill for a woman to earn a GED during her tenure with us.

Chalina had a third-grade reading level when she started working with us. Not surprising—she essentially stopped attending school around fifth or sixth grade, when she was kicked out of her mother's home. Her mom had already introduced her to cocaine and then saw Chalina as competition for boyfriends. I never met her mom, but Chalina was lovely, with long, golden hair and sparkling blue eyes.

I could imagine how the kind of guys Chalina's mom hung out with would have been interested in the pretty young girl. For Chalina, the right educational solution was to wait until she graduated from Women's Bean Project and got a job. She then enrolled in a remedial adult high school. She knew it would take her years to catch up, but she was motivated because she believed in the power of education to create opportunity for herself.

Dropping out of school is a chicken-and-egg dilemma. Those who come from a poor family are more likely to drop out of school. And dropping out of school makes one more likely to be poor. Which comes first? One thing is for sure: for many of the women at the Bean Project, dropping out of school was the first of many missteps that ultimately led them to us.

In hindsight, I see that the young woman at the Spot was on her way to becoming a client of Women's Bean Project. She likely had already run away from home—which is common for the kids at the Spot—trying to escape a bad, possibly abusive, home. She likely had fallen into an even worse situation on the streets. Yet, someone had helped her understand that a GED was one of the three keys to getting out of poverty. I hoped she would avoid teenage pregnancy and single parenthood and find a full-time job, though the former seemed more likely to happen than the latter. Perhaps this young woman would first apply for welfare to support herself while she was trying to find one of the menial jobs for which she was qualified, starting the ticking sixty-month clock on welfare benefits.

I wondered if this young woman had ever had much of a chance. I assumed she had grown up in poverty, like many of the women at the Bean Project. Literacy experts confirm that two-thirds of American children living in poverty don't have access to books, leading to lower reading achievement. These children with below-grade-level reading skills are twice as likely to drop out of school. In turn, research has shown a link between reading problems and aggressive, even violent, behavior. Seventy percent of incarcerated adults have low literacy skills.

Jessie dropped out of school when she ran away from home at fourteen. By the time she was hired at the Bean Project, she was in her early thirties and had lived on the street for fifteen years. Like most of the women at the Bean Project, Jessie was a single parent, but in her case to fraternal twins. The twins were not Jessie's first children. She'd had a daughter several years earlier when she was still an addict. As a result of Jessie's drug use during her first pregnancy, her daughter had severe emotional and behavioral issues that set her at least two years behind developmentally. Jessie continued to be caught up in her addiction even after the birth of her first daughter and had signed away parental rights to allow her mother, the baby's grandmother, to adopt the baby.

Jessie saw her second pregnancy as her opportunity to make up for her prior mistakes, and she chose to go to the Haven, a residential drug treatment and alternative to incarceration. The advantage of the Haven is that residents are able to have their children with them while they work through treatment and fulfill their correctional sentence. Jessie didn't plan to be a single parent, but the twins' father died from a heroin and alcohol overdose before their birth. By the time Jessie was hired by the Bean Project, she was almost finished with her program at the Haven, her twins were nearly two years old and she was figuring out how to support her family of three.

Like most women we hire, Jessie didn't have a car. Even if she'd had a driver's license—she'd lost hers as a result of her convictions and outstanding fines—she didn't have the funds to purchase a reliable car, much less the gas, insurance, and upkeep. The stereotype of a welfare recipient who drives a fancy car and wears expensive clothing is far outside my observation. Jessie was a case in point. She used a double stroller and public transportation to take her toddlers from home to daycare, and back each day.

One day, Jessie arrived at work late and visibly shaken. She described how the day had started out normally, with her and the twins taking light-rail to daycare. During one of the switches to another train, Jessie placed both toddlers into the double-wide stroller. While she strapped in her daughter, her son rolled out of the stroller, across the platform and nearly onto the track. Jessie moved quickly and gathered her son who was only startled. It was an unnerving close call.

Many employers wouldn't tolerate the unreliability of Jessie's life, and although her life wouldn't always be as hectic as it was with toddler twins, she needed to establish herself in order to create a life for her family that extended beyond mere survival.

So often single parenthood traps women in poverty by creating unavoidable paradoxes. Landlords don't like to rent to single moms because they don't want the risk. Kids get sick and single moms have no one to stay home with them, so they lose wages and sometimes even their job. Women with no child care are unable to find a job, and they can't afford child care without a job. Often the women have low skill levels and can work only limited hours, so they are qualified only for such low-wage jobs that they are hardly better off being employed.

Girls born to teen parents are almost 33 percent more likely to become teen parents themselves, continuing the cycle of dropping out of school and living in poverty. I wonder how it is ever possible for someone to overcome these odds and change the course of events. Most of the women at the Bean Project gave birth to their first child while in their teens. Many of them grew up in poverty, only to repeat the cycle as adults.

Jessie was smart and well-spoken, from a white, middle-class family on Long Island. At fourteen, when she ran away from her father's rules, she began a fifteen-year odyssey of addiction and homelessness. Though she could easily have handled it intellectually, Jessie had never learned about computers, which became commonplace while she lived on the streets. As she would say with her toothless smile (she had dentures, but not the money to get them fitted properly), "The entire computer age just passed me by. I have a lot of catching up to do." Until Jessie developed her skills, she would struggle to get a job that tapped her capacity and made it possible to support her twins.

Children can be the barriers for a mother's employment. Meredith had never been in trouble, but she dropped out of school when she had her first child at seventeen. She and the child's father later got married and had two more kids. By the time she landed at the Bean, she was in her forties and tired of struggling. Yet, she always came to work with makeup applied and her long, dark hair piled on top of her head, ready for a hairnet. While they never had a lot of money, the situation became unmanageable when Meredith and her husband divorced, leaving her to support all three children. Meredith had not developed job skills, but we learned that she was a good worker who brought a positive attitude and eagerness to work each day. As she neared the end of the program and began preparing for her transition to permanent, full-time employment, one of her sons wreaked havoc on her plans. While Meredith was at work, the son and his cousin entered the laundry room of their apartment building and tore it apart, vandalizing it to the point that none of the machines were operational. Besides wanting to press charges for vandalism, the landlord wanted them to immediately leave the building. Meredith scrambled. She did not have enough money for a deposit on a new apartment, for surely she would lose the one she had set down on her current apartment. She had only a few days to find affordable housing, and the current landlord was not going to provide a reference for her. Meredith, the reliable employee, suddenly began missing work frequently and began to fall below the ninety percent attendance threshold to be in good standing for her job at the Bean Project. Though barely, she maintained her job with us until she found another, but the new job was only part-time because she couldn't manage her son and work full-time. I wondered how she was going to afford an apartment and other living expenses on part-time pay.

And this part-time job would preclude access to a portion of her assistance. I used to think that people on welfare didn't want to work—didn't want to try to work might be the way I would have said it. Like many people, I believed that we had created a welfare state that encouraged individuals to stay in the welfare system for generation after generation. I recall being encouraged when, in 1996, President Clinton signed into law the Personal Responsibility and Work Reconciliation Act, or what is commonly known as the Welfare Reform Act, to create welfare-to-work programs. While I didn't know the specifics, I appreciated that this reform discouraged lifetime, multigenerational system-milking. The act changed the name of welfare to Temporary Assistance for Needy Families

(TANF) and created a sixty-month lifetime limit for benefits. No longer would individuals be able to stay on welfare forever. There was a cutoff to ensure a transition to employment.

By the time I started working at the Bean Project in 2003, much of the benefit of the new policy was evident. Before the law's enactment, twelve million people were on welfare. By 2001, only five million people were. During the first ten years of welfare reform, child poverty fell, especially for black children. Additionally, the poverty rate for single moms fell dramatically. More mothers were going to work.

Those who remain in the system are the kind of women who arrive at the Bean Project. They have significant, complex and layered barriers to employment. They lack basic needs such as housing, transportation, child care and health care. Their education is poor and their skill levels low. And they are caught in the trap of unemployability based on lack of employment history and no knowledge of the basic agreements employees and employers enter into when someone is hired. While I still agree with a lifetime limit to benefits, I recognize that for the women coming to the Bean Project, there is a gap between welfare ending and the ability to go to work. Women's Bean Project is now dealing with those who are the hardest to serve, those who tried—often multiple times—to create new lives for themselves and their families, but failed because of addiction, mental illness, felony convictions, domestic violence and myriad other issues, none of which occur alone.

Those remaining on the welfare rolls are "hard to employ," meaning they face a broad range of obstacles to employment, such as lacking a high school diploma or GED, having limited work experience, having been exposed to domestic violence, having substance abuse or mental health problems, or having limited English skills. Many people who face these and other problems are unable to find and sustain employment, requiring targeted assistance to help them become self-sufficient, including supported-employment environments.

In No One is Unemployable, Debra Angel and Elisabeth Harney work from the assumption that no one has barriers that will excuse them entirely from employment. They focus on identifying barriers, understanding the perspectives of the employer and the job candidate regarding the barrier, and then working with the job candidate to develop effective solutions that will satisfy the employer. Women's Bean Project staff and some case managers with whom Women's Bean Project works are trained in this philosophy, providing the mindset and tools for overcoming barriers. Subsequently, the biggest challenge all case managers face is finding workplaces willing to accept clients like the graduates of Women's Bean Project. Many employers will not even consider employing someone with a criminal background, regardless of how much time has passed since their offense. If a woman can move from welfare to work and begin a career entry-level job (our stated goal), her struggle doesn't end. Perhaps more relevant than the federal poverty level is the self-sufficiency standard, which defines the income a family needs to meet their basic needs without any assistance. The self-sufficiency standard for Denver County in 2008, for a family with one adult, one preschooler and one school-age child, required a minimum wage of $19.66 per hour, or two and a half times the requirement to meet the federal poverty level. Women who graduated from the Bean Project in 2012 earned an average wage of $10.50. Because of their backgrounds, education level, work experience and criminal histories, to name just a few of the factors influencing their pay, it will be a long time—if ever—before these women come anywhere close to the self-sufficiency standard. And even as they make progress, the system often will continue to work against them.

Traci, one of our hourly staff members whom we hired to supervise jewelry production, had formerly been on welfare. Her workforce development counselor connected her with the Bean Project to help her transition to permanent employment. She had a very sweet demeanor and a nice smile of straight, white teeth, but hid behind a tough appearance with multiple tattoos and piercings. Finding mainstream employment was going to be difficult because many employers would struggle to get past her physical characteristics. She had a GED and a work history that included a few steady jobs. She'd been slowly making her way into stability and was extremely grateful for the job at the Bean Project that moved her up the pay scale. But her wage still necessitated that she receive assistance for subsidized housing and utilities. One winter, on a snowy afternoon, she used paid time off to go to the office of the Low Income Energy Assistance Program (LEAP) to apply for help with her heating bill. She was required to present her pay stubs to demonstrate her need. After a cursory review of her paperwork, the counselor pushed the papers back across the desk, informing Traci she made just one dollar too much to qualify for assistance. Traci had been counting on this help to get herself and her son through the frigid winter months. The counselor saw her disappointment and made a suggestion. If she could miss just one day of work in the next pay period and bring in that pay stub, the counselor would be able to help her qualify for the assistance.

Traci returned to the office dejected and seeking advice. She sat in the chair next to my desk without removing her coat as if the news had given her a chill she couldn't shake and asked what I thought she should do. I appreciated the counselor's creativity, though I wondered about a system that created such backward incentives without taking into account all of the ramifications. If Traci followed the counselor's suggestion, it would impact her ability to cover other expenses like groceries or gas for her car. As taxpayers, we say we want people to get off welfare, get jobs and pay their own way. Yet, as taxpayers we endorse programs that create disincentives for just such behavior. As the employer, I didn't want to hear that the LEAP counselor was encouraging a member of our staff to miss work without pay. But I did want to ensure Traci had access to all of the benefits she needed to thrive.

In a study titled *Two Steps Forward and Three Steps Back*, the Women's Foundation of Colorado describes the Cliff Effect— Colorado's Curious Penalty for Increased Earnings. This quantitative analysis highlights a disincentive to improve pay. Many low-income families receive benefits (e.g., earned income tax credits, Medicaid, child care assistance) to help cover the cost of basic necessities, but, as earnings increase, families begin to lose these benefits. Benefit cliffs can mean that an increase in earnings may not improve a family's financial situation. Even in the best cases, the earnings increase, but the family is only marginally better off. In the worst case, parents can work more and earn more, but their families end up worse off financially because they are no longer eligible to receive certain benefits that help bridge gaps between their income and expenses.

I was curious what the women at the Bean Project thought of the welfare regulations. "The most frustrating part is the paperwork and scrutiny that comes with getting assistance," said one. "You might not be aware there is a problem, until suddenly you don't get funded."

Like Janine, most of the women need monthly food assistance. A month or so after talking with Janine, I went back to the shipping department to ask more questions about how she made $150 in food stamps work for a family of five. As usual, when I told her I had more questions, she smiled and warmly agreed. We stepped to the side of the shipping area and stood near a tall shelf stocked with Bean Project products.

"Can you tell me more about how you make $150 a month in food stamps work for your family?" I asked.

Janine's face crumpled, "Well, two days ago I went for redetermination—you have to do that every six months—and they decreased me to twenty-one dollars."

"A month? Janine, how did that happen?"

"I don't know. Even with my garnishment, when they put everything into the computer, it came out to be twenty-one dollars. I don't know what I'm going to do." She began to tear up.

I reached to her through the shelf to touch her arm. "Oh, Janine. I'm sorry." I was beginning to cry too. It didn't occur to me at the time, but I suppose it was ironic that we were standing next to a shelf full of food talking about Janine's loss of access to food.

She wiped away the tears with her thumb and jutted her chin forward. "I'm not going backward. That's why I'm taking every overtime hour offered here. Every extra dollar on my check helps me."

"Have you talked to Lisa?" Lisa was our case manager and the staff member who helped the women with problems such as these. "And what about your garnishment? Can you get that decreased?"

I mentally scrambled to think of possible solutions. I didn't want to see Janine fail. I truly believed she was doing everything right.

"I've applied again to change my garnishments. They denied me the first time. Then you have to wait thirty days to apply again, so I did, but I haven't heard. But the first time I heard right away and this time it's taking a while, so maybe that's a good sign." That seemed like a lot to count on when she couldn't feed her kids.

"Can you go back to the people who determine the garnishments and tell them your food stamps were cut?" I imagined that the various systems didn't communicate and they depended on Janine to tell them when something changed.

"I don't know. I just found out, so I haven't done anything yet." I could feel her helpless desperation. "I haven't even told my kids yet, but I haven't bought groceries this month." It was the ninth of the month. "We don't have any food at home. I need to do something, but I don't want to spend the twenty-one dollars since it's all I have for the whole month."

"Can you send your son to the food pantry so you don't have to miss work?" Typically the pantries were open during work hours, and I knew that Janine had just missed a couple of hours to get a drug test that was a condition of her parole.

"You have to be eighteen to go to the pantries. He'll be eighteen next month." That triggered Janine to remember, "My landlord just called me to the office and told me that my rent will have to go up when my son turns eighteen since there will be two adults in the apartment. But I am going to appeal that since he's a full-time student."

I could feel the avalanche on Janine's behalf. Janine wasn't the first woman I'd known to have these problems. Jessie also had experienced a problem with her food stamps. One day during our regular morning meeting, Jessie had said her personal goal that week was to go to the food stamps office. "They suddenly lowered my food stamps from $561 per month to $31. I will have to miss a day of work to stand in line to find out why."

When Jessie returned from lunch one afternoon, I met her near her locker and asked her about the visit to the food stamp office. The problem turned out to be her former employer. "Everything has to be done electronically now, and they refused to e-verify that I was no longer employed there because it costs them money to do the e-verification." As a result, the food stamps office assumed Jessie had two jobs and didn't need the same level of support as she had previously received. The income verification was required each month. Paperwork was lost frequently. "You must keep your own paper trail," Jessie emphasized. It reaffirmed the importance of the planning and organizing class we offer the women at the Bean Project.

I walked with Jessie back to the jewelry production table, and several of the women chimed in on our conversation, providing a mini–food stamp tutorial. I asked if it was embarrassing to get food stamps. I could recall being at grocery stores when someone ahead of me in line used food stamps. It always slowed down the process, and I had noticed the irritation displayed by the cashiers. "This used to be true," the women confirmed, "but now your Quest card is funded, and you get notified by text message when the money is available." The old food stamps did take longer to use, the line was held up and people would notice. The card changed all that. It worked just like any other debit card.

I was surprised when Jessie and her colleagues, as they sat at the table making jewelry, agreed that drug tests should be a condition for getting assistance. "If you aren't clean, you aren't really making the effort to change, so you shouldn't be able to get assistance. Let's save it for someone who really wants to make their life better." They all would have suffered the consequences of this policy in the past. Each woman's survival depended on her ability to follow the rules of a human services system that appeared to me to be designed to dehumanize her. Yet they were defending the system.

What is the answer to helping people break out of poverty? I watch so many single mothers struggle and know that, aside from the fact that I have a higher income, my life is much easier because I have a husband with whom I share parenting responsibilities. But encouraging the women to get married isn't the solution. Within poor communities of color, as many as one-third of all black men are incarcerated. Even if they are inclined to get married, many women wouldn't find enough men in their communities to find a husband.

With two drug-addicted parents, did Janine have a chance at not repeating the cycle? Women like Janine are often stuck in circumstances that are beyond their control. That is the poverty trap, the cycle that keeps people in poverty even when they try to lift themselves up. The Brookings Institute emphasizes that programs that ultimately lift someone out of poverty don't just address an immediate need, but also address the underlying causes and enable them to become self-sufficient for the rest of their lives and, ideally, for generations after them.

Poverty often extends for generations. Working at the Bean Project, I see intergenerational poverty right before my eyes. Through the years I have met women, then their mothers, sisters, aunts and cousins: multiple generations, across family units, all living in poverty. Statistically, growing up in poverty nearly guarantees that a child will live in poverty as an adult. Economists describe the cycle of poverty as the "set of factors or events by which poverty, once started, is likely to continue unless there is outside intervention." It is a phenomenon in which poor families become trapped in poverty for at least three generations, creating a family atmosphere in which there are no living family members who know what it is like not to live in poverty. In these families there are limited or no resources, such as financial capital, education and connections. These disadvantages work together in a circular process, making it virtually impossible for individuals to break out.

We will hire a woman at the Bean Project. Then, in the next group, we will hire her sister. Later, I will learn that their aunt is now in the program and that another woman who had been in the program was a cousin. In these families poverty, addiction and incarceration are pervasive across family units and generations.

Alicia's mom was never there for her when she was growing up. While their mother cycled in and out of prison, Erin and her siblings were raised by family members and learned to fend for themselves at young ages. When she started working at the Bean Project, Alicia was living in the halfway house where she had been sentenced in lieu of prison for burglary. She had a quick, gap-toothed smile that faded whenever she talked about her sister. Alicia's sister had spent time in prison and was in the same halfway house. I was picking up my mail one day at the front desk where Alicia worked when she told me why she worried about her sister: "She just keeps blaming everyone else. She can't see that everything that has happened to her is her own responsibility." Shortly after that, Alicia's sister ran from the halfway house. Meanwhile, Alicia stayed the course and was eventually released to live in the community. When Alicia's mother saw her success, she applied to work at the Bean Project. But Alicia's achievements were the family anomaly. We eventually fired Alicia's mom for a positive drug test. Later we heard from Alicia that both her mom and her sister were back in prison.

Tara was the kind of person I thought represented most people in poverty. She came to the Bean Project when she was in her late twenties because she'd been unable to keep a job to support herself and her four-year-old daughter. Tara's mother had referred her, recognizing that the Bean Project could help Tara build skills and address the issues she'd had with keeping employment. Tara's mom accompanied her to the Bean Project on her first visit. Her mother knew from experience that the program worked; she'd been a program participant at the Bean a dozen years earlier. In Tara's mother's case, the program facilitated a long-term change that enabled her to move off welfare and into a job with the school district where she had stayed since her graduation.

Tara had one advantage many women hired by the Bean Project don't; she had no felony background. But she wasn't able to tell us why she struggled to maintain employment and get off of welfare.

I remember warming to Tara immediately. When she came to work, she was always upbeat with a put-together look that often included a cute blazer. Tara was a bright spot at every morning meeting and so delightful that I initially had trouble believing her work history. During her intake interview she indicated that her primary goal was to pursue a career in fashion after graduation. She was so determined that she began taking classes in fashion design at a local art school. We assigned her to the gift basket production area, hoping that it would provide an outlet for her artistic flair and satisfy her creative desire.

Everything went well for a couple of months. Her attendance was great, and she was a bright spot on the production floor. Then she began to meddle, but not in a harmless way. Identifying vulnerabilities in her coworkers, she would repeat confidential information, strategically share inappropriate facts and generally wreak havoc on the interpersonal dynamics between her fellow gift basket makers. We were surprised, though we probably shouldn't have been. There was a reason Tara had struggled to maintain employment, even though it took us a while to see it. No one had ever taught Tara appropriate workplace—or even life—behavior and attitudes.

Joyce was a counselor we hired to teach the women, through group sessions, about interpersonal communications, personal responsibility and positive life outlook. All of the women enjoyed Joyce, and some sought her counsel outside of the Bean Project. Her gentle demeanor had a Mother Earth quality. When she led her group sessions, she'd stand in the center of the room, posing questions and managing the spirited conversation that ensued. She always smiled and spoke softly. For Tara in particular, something about these group sessions clicked even more than for the other women. She did an about-face and kept to herself unless she had something positive to say or do. She concentrated on her long-term goal of working in fashion and began to identify possible opportunities with a vigor we didn't know she had in her. We moved Tara to another work area where she took on team-leader responsibilities. As it came closer to her time to graduate and move to employment in the community, Tara was effusive about how Joyce had helped her. "I know you all call these life skills, but I call them life savers." She went on to describe how she finally saw that she alone had control over her own behavior and response to others. She didn't need to worry about others' actions. They were responsible for themselves, and she could choose not to engage.

Tara needed to understand how her own behavior was trapping her in poverty. I hoped the life change had come early enough to affect her daughter. She was only four years old, and there was a chance she could grow up and remember only a mother who worked and provided for her.

For many people, poverty remains complex and multi-dimensional. In *Skill and Will*, David Shipler argues that poverty has many related issues and that focusing on just one aspect of poverty—like housing—will not effect change. Poverty, in Shipler's view, is a "constellation of difficulties that magnify one another: not just low wages but also low education, not just dead-end jobs but also limited abilities, not just insufficient savings but also unwise spending, not just poor housing but also poor parenting, not just the lack of health insurance but also the lack of healthy households."

Janine, along with her fellow program participants at the Bean Project, worked hard to change their lives and break the cycle of poverty for their children. The participants have full-time jobs, and many are working on their education and want to get their children back and keep their families together. But every time I hear a story about how the system conspires against them, I worry. Will there be a time when they decide it isn't worth all the effort, that the boulder is just too big to push uphill?

CHAPTER 4

FREEDOM'S JUST ANOTHER WORD— HOW THE CRIMINAL JUSTICE SYSTEM WORKS AGAINST REHABILITATION

One Tuesday morning, after missing work the previous day, Shayla walked into the Bean Project. When I hadn't seen her in morning meeting the day before, I'd asked about her and was told she hadn't called in. I was surprised Shayla would miss work, especially without calling. She was in the middle of a job search and had been on a few interviews, which placed her on the verge of graduating. That Tuesday, I pulled her aside and asked how she was. She was several inches taller than I, so I looked up into her dark eyes. She shook her head and said when she'd arrived at the halfway house after work on Friday, she was told she was on lockdown. She wouldn't be allowed to leave the facility until she met with her case manager and therapist on Monday. The lockdown meant she lost the weekend pass she'd earned that allowed her to visit to her kids, would have to miss work on Monday and had lost her telephone privileges and so could not notify her kids or the Bean Project. Lockdowns typically are imposed for behavioral issues such as a disrespectful interaction with halfway house staff. But from what I'd seen, Shayla had a good attitude and was working hard to get out of the halfway house and reunite with her kids.

Shayla appeared frazzled. She described how she'd spent the weekend wondering what was wrong while no one at the halfway house would tell her anything other than to wait until the meeting on Monday. Without knowing what she'd done to deserve the lockdown, Shayla was on edge, disappointed that she was unable to visit her kids and frustrated that she couldn't call to let them know she wouldn't be coming. "The halfway house said they'd called to tell you I wouldn't be in on Monday," Shayla told me. But no one had called us so Shayla received the first of three strikes on our no-call-no-show policy.

When she finally sat down with halfway house staff members in a small room, they said a fellow resident had reported that Shayla was bullying her. Shayla was shocked and didn't know what they were talking about. A heated conversation ensued, and one of the staff members told her, "Well, this attitude is to be expected, based on your background."

Shayla was floored by what she interpreted as a racial remark—in her mind the only difference between her and other women in the halfway house was skin color. "Excuse me?" she said, then went on to tell the staff that although she was black, she grew up in a middle-class home, had attended Catholic school, then a predominantly white high school. Shayla said the meeting ended with her walking out of the room.

As I listened to her story, I wondered if the staff had been trying to push Shayla to act out. I'd heard other women, as they approached their "out dates," the designated day for release from the halfway house, tell stories of how the staff tried to bait them into getting angry by assigning extra cleaning chores or giving what the women perceived as unfair or arbitrary punishment for infractions that might have previously been ignored. If I'd heard about each case in isolation, I might not have believed it, but I heard these stories consistently enough that I realized there must be some truth to it. I grabbed Shayla's hand to get her attention and said softly, "Don't prove them right. If they are trying to make you mad and they have an expectation about how you'll act, don't give them the satisfaction of being correct." She nodded, but I wasn't sure the comment had sunk in.

From Shayla's experience—and those of countless other women I've met over the years—I've learned that freedom is not the only thing taken away when a woman is convicted of a crime. I have learned how the corrections system dehumanizes women, how the checks and balances intended to ensure that felons follow the rules can feel arbitrary and how basic human respect is often denied. These forces leave the women struggling to regain their humanity and self-respect before they can function in the community again.

Most of the women I meet at the Bean Project experience all three phases of the corrections system: prison, halfway houses and parole. By the time I meet them, the majority of our employees have spent time—sometimes over the course of several sentences—in prison. Prisons in America originally were intended to remove individuals who are a threat to society, ensuring public welfare and safety by isolating those who threaten that safety. Between 1977 and 2004, female imprisonment increased 757 percent, making prisons more like overstuffed warehouses. Prison overcrowding is the extreme in dehumanization.

Overcrowding leads to increased stress, blood pressure, and sleep deprivation. Overcrowded prisons fail to offer the educational and rehabilitative programs they were intended to provide inmates to help them return to productive lives on the outside. In general, locking people up makes them feel anonymous and rejected by society. The prison system reinforces these feelings by assigning inmates numbers, requiring them to wear the same uniform, and taking away or severely limiting personal possessions. Felons retain those numbers until they are "killed," or their sentence is completed entirely, often long after their release from prison. Inmates feel inadequate, rejected and undesirable, and doubt their ability to contribute to society. By the time women arrive at the Bean Project, they have internalized these feelings of low self-esteem. While they know they aren't dangerous—less than 18 percent of women are incarcerated for violent crimes—they do buy into the notion that they are undesirable. Our employees' low self-esteem often manifests in an unwillingness to look me in the eye when we meet, a closed-down posture and an angry demeanor—something I've learned to recognize as a defense mechanism. During our program, as the women begin to accomplish goals and feel safe, these qualities begin to disappear.

A well-known psychological experiment conducted at Stanford University in 1971 illustrates how human nature interacts with the prison environment to make dehumanizing behavior the norm. In the Stanford experiment, twenty-four volunteers were randomly assigned to be either prisoners or guards in a make-shift prison created in the basement of one of the campus buildings. Prior to making the random assignments, researchers evaluated all of the volunteers to ensure none had psychological problems, medical disabilities or histories of crime or drug abuse. The final group of twenty-four participants in the study were healthy, intelligent, middle-class young men.

During their orientation, the guard volunteers were instructed not to physically harm the prisoners, but they were told it was okay to create boredom, fear and the feeling of arbitrariness that the prisoners' lives were totally controlled by the guards and the system.

The prisoner volunteers were arrested and processed through the local police department just as any felon would be. When sent to prison, they were assigned numbers that became their sole means of identification.

The experiment, set to last two weeks, was cut short after only six days because both the guards and the prisoners devolved into behavior that was not predicted by the psychological tests administered prior to the experiment. Prisoners quickly began to feel and act powerless and hopeless. By the end of the experiment the prisoners displayed no group unity; they were merely a group of individuals trying to cope with the situation.

The guards, however, pulled together to exert authority and control over the prisoners, and ended up falling evenly into three categories: guards who were tough but fair; guards who were good guys, doing favors for the prisoners and not punishing them; and guards who became hostile toward the prisoners, creating progressively more innovative ways to punish them.

As the study suggests, there is something innate in human behavior that allows humans in a position of power to treat others inhumanely when others have little or limited power and control. Prisoners become passive and depressed under such strains.

According to Human Rights Watch, a nongovernmental organization, mistreatment of prisoners is a tradition. The justice system has found on more than one occasion that prison environments are pervaded by cultures of abuse, sadism and malice. Solitary confinement frequently is used as punishment within the prison. Bean Project participants often tell me about their fear of landing in the "hole" — twenty-three-hour-a-day solitary confinement.

Prisons impose extreme stresses on inmates, but the stresses don't end when a woman is released. The Bureau of Prisons contracts with residential reentry centers, also known as halfway houses, to provide assistance to inmates who are nearing release. Halfway houses were developed as a way station between prison and the community, a means to reintegrate former inmates into the community by providing support and monitoring. With prison overcrowding and the annual cost of incarceration that can exceed $60,000 per person, per year, community corrections has become an essential part of the system. There just isn't enough money in states' budgets to incarcerate the glut of felons created by stricter drug sentencing laws. To defray the costs of long-term detention, residents of halfway houses pay for room and board and other services, such as classes and drug tests they are required to take. Halfway houses are intended to provide a safe, structured and supervised environment while ensuring public safety by restricting the freedom of offenders, continuing to hold them accountable for their crimes and addressing characteristics that have led to their criminal activity, such as addiction and joblessness.

While these goals are admirable, the halfway house system can be harsh. Halfway houses are less structured and restrictive than prison, but they still have extensive rules, and the threat of being sent back to prison for breaking these rules always hangs over the residents' heads. As one of our employees once told me, "In the halfway house, they give you enough rope to hang yourself." On the one hand, halfway houses can assist former prisoners with reintegration into communities, helping to ensure they stay clean and get jobs while trying to re-engage with society. However, our program participants have shared numerous stories about their experiences with staff members that lead me to believe some halfway houses are operated better and more fairly than others. The halfway houses we interact with are run by private companies that benefit financially from released prisoners being sentenced to their facilities.

Program participants frequently complain about how some halfway house staff members exert their power by imposing rules unevenly, like choosing who is required to perform distasteful chores, like cleaning the bathrooms, on the basis of personal preference. They often are frustrated at how a halfway house punishes all for the actions of one. For example, the entire facility will be locked down and no one allowed to go to work or use their weekend passes if someone runs away or brings in contraband, such as food.

In the halfway house, women must function in a weird in-between world. They live with restrictions, threats and penalties, while being expected to participate in the community by finding a job and paying for their stay. Halfway houses are a sort of limbo, a curious place between freedom and incarceration, free but not free—free to make the mistakes that remove the freedom they desperately seek and accountable for every moment of each day.

I stood by the Bean's employee entrance one morning, greeting the women as they walked in. A few minutes before 8:00, the time all program participants are required to arrive for work, Samantha walked in, laughing. Upon crossing the threshold, and without removing her jacket, she walked to the phone, picked up the receiver and began to dial. I watched her face, flush from the frigid late autumn air, become serious. When the phone was answered on the other end, she said flatly, "Ms. Sanchez, this is Wilson making my arrival call at Women's Bean Project." Then she handed the receiver to the next woman, who handed it to the next, and so on, until all six women who had arrived together from the same halfway house repeated the drill. While making the call, they huddled in somber solidarity. As soon as the call ended, they walked in unison a few feet to the computer monitor where they clocked in for work, resuming their conversation, smiles and laughter.

Calling the halfway house is a twice-a-day ritual for women living in one. When it is time to leave the Bean Project for the day, every resident is required to call the halfway house to notify them she is leaving to walk to the bus stop. This gives the halfway house staff an idea of when they can expect the women to return to the facility. Not only are halfway house residents not allowed to leave the workplace during the day, they are punished with a write-up if they exit the bus en route. Write-ups are serious infractions that result in loss of privileges and, potentially, a return to prison.

The halfway house where Samantha and many other program participants are sentenced is across some railroad tracks in a warehouse district, an apt location since the building itself looks a lot like a warehouse. No one would want a halfway house near their home, so this may have been the best location the halfway house operators could secure. It is a two-story building that appears to be made with little other than sheet metal, but closer inspection reveals that concrete blocks are its primary building material. Nothing about the building appears warm or welcoming. It is a stopping point for women who are still being punished.

Inside the halfway house, the women sleep on bunk beds, six or eight to a room, each on a four-inch single mattress, the same kind found in prison. With so many women in one room, it is not surprising there are disagreements and conflicts, such as what Shayla experienced. It doesn't matter if the women in a particular room don't get along; they won't get a different assignment, even if they ask.

The women are allowed to have some of their own possessions while in the halfway house. For instance, they can have an alarm clock, and if purchased from the Department of Corrections it is made of clear plastic, as are the televisions they can buy from the prison commissary. The DOC reckons that people can't hide things in clear alarm clocks or televisions.

Every resident has a tall, rectangular locker where she keeps all of her belongings. They are allowed to have shampoo and other personal hygiene items purchased from a nearby Wal-Mart when they are allowed to leave the facility on a two-hour hygiene pass. This is the only kind of pass women are allowed early in their tenure at the halfway house and can only be used for a trip to Wal-Mart and only for personal hygiene items. Their bags are inspected when they return.

All items for the shower have to be taken down the hall to a bathroom with eight stalls. Then, each woman can choose the day's outfit from the thirty-six articles of clothing she is allowed. After getting ready for the day, the women have breakfast, which consists of cold, dry cereal—according to the halfway house residents, the milk is often spoiled. There also is a fruit bowl, but everything is usually overripe. Then, on her way out the front door, each woman grabs her sack lunch and lines up for checkout. Checkout times must be approved based on the halfway house's confirmation of the time the woman is due at work.

The women's sack lunches are the same every day—two mushy, white-bread sandwiches with bologna, salami or ham; one small, mealy apple (though sometimes it is an orange); graham crackers; and a juice box. Halfway house residents sit at a table in the Bean Project kitchen quietly while other women, those who aren't in halfway houses, bring leftovers from home, or they leave the Bean Project premises to purchase food from a local fast-food restaurant like the dollar-a-scoop meal from the local Chinese restaurant down the street. Not a healthy choice, but the halfway house women envy their ability to eat whatever they choose.

During morning meeting, program participants living in halfway houses often make reference to paying their back rent. Back rent refers to the debt that accrues between the time a woman first arrives at the halfway house and when she finds a job, often as long as two or three months. During this pre-employment period, women are referred to as indigent residents and are subject to numerous indignities: they are relegated to the seldom-operating indigent washer and dryer and forced to borrow money for bus fare from fellow residents to secretly meet a family member or to fund a job search. But only ten dollars—indigent residents are not allowed to carry more. Although the halfway house staff is supposed to have a supply of bus tokens for the indigent residents looking for a job, they aren't provided. If help from a family member isn't available, women struggle to get bus fare and the change needed for a pay phone to make the required check-in calls to the halfway house while applying for a job. Women aren't allowed to be out of the halfway house all day without proof they are looking for work. Prospective employers must sign a form to confirm that a woman has applied for a job at their business. A phone call to the halfway house when she is leaving the potential employer ensures the halfway house knows where she is at all times. But some employers don't allow visitors to use their phones, and often residents don't want the draw an employer's attention to their living situation by asking to borrow the phone. Having to ask the potential employer to verify she was there feels bad enough; finding a pay phone to call in can be downright impossible.

Why not use a cell phone, you ask? Because halfway house residents aren't allowed to have cell phones until they earn the privilege by getting a job, paying off their debt, staying current with rent and participating in the required treatment classes. When women are approved for a cell phone, it must be a prepaid account and cannot contain more than twenty dollars of credit at a time. While there is a pay phone at the halfway house that residents can use for limited outgoing calls, no incoming calls are allowed. If residents' families are out of town, residents must call collect. Women often have cell phones anyway, which they frequently hide in their cleavages.

Women typically complete dozens of applications before they find a job. Not many employers will hire a felon, much less a felon with minimal work experience like the women who find their way to the Bean Project. Women with a high school diploma have a small advantage, but only about half of the women we hire have graduated from high school.

During this job search, halfway house residents incur debt for their room and board, as well as for drug tests and treatment classes. Room and board costs seventeen dollars a day. Women are also ordered to take weekly classes, based on their criminal conviction, such as anger management and drug treatment. The cost ranges from twelve dollars to twenty-five dollars each. Drug tests, also required and performed randomly, cost fifteen dollars. Individually, these fees don't seem like a lot until they begin to rack up without a means for paying. By the time women start working at the Bean Project, they typically are a few thousand dollars in debt.

Once she has secures employment, each woman is required to sign over her pay check to the halfway house staff when she arrives at the halfway house on payday. The penalty for not doing so is a return trip to prison. The net amounts of the women's paychecks are not impressive. We are required to garnish the wages of most women, typically to cover foster care costs while a woman was in prison or restitution for the financial impact of her crimes. Women we employ at the Bean Project have an average of three children, so there often are garnishments for each child individually, and often the various entities aren't aware that there are other garnishment notices. So the garnishments compound, sometimes leaving very little in a woman's net pay.

One payday, I walked into Luanne's, our controller's, office, inadvertently interrupting an impromptu meeting she was having with Veronica, a program participant who had received her first paycheck, from which garnishments for foster care expenses had been taken. I could see Veronica was crying and shot a curious look to Luanne. She explained that she and Veronica had just been talking about alternatives available to Veronica for challenging or reducing her garnishments and increasing her take-home pay. At the time, as a result of the four garnishments, her net paycheck was only forty-five dollars for a two-week pay period. Veronica said she understood why she needed to pay back the cost of taking care of her kids while she was in prison, but she wondered why she should work if she was going to give so much from each check that she couldn't pay her bills. The net amount of each biweekly paycheck is applied toward the current rent and the remainder is applied to the resident's halfway house debt. It is always cause for celebration in morning meeting when a woman announces she's "caught up in her rent," meaning she's finished paying back her debt to the halfway house. This can take many months. If a program participant works all of the hours available to her, the net pay every two weeks, without garnishments, is typically about $450. Her rent, treatment classes and drug tests can cost as much as $350 every two weeks. After the cost of basic personal supplies are deducted, less than $100 per pay period remains to apply toward her debt. As a result, a debt of $3,000 in back rent can require nearly a year to pay down.

After rent is caught up, a halfway house resident continues to sign over her paychecks, but the amount remaining after restitution, rent and treatment classes goes into savings, ready and waiting for her when she finally gets paroled and moves into her own apartment.

In addition to meeting the requirements of good behavior and attitude, as well as keeping a full-time job, each woman is required to have saved at least $500 to be eligible for parole. However, she typically needs to save more. When she is finally granted parole, she must first find an affordable apartment that will accept her despite her background, have enough money saved to pay a deposit, then have at least $500 remaining in savings. Because many landlords consider these women high-risk tenants, they often are required to provide large deposits, several times the monthly rent. Again, the financial hurdles a woman must clear to gain her freedom are imposing and often overwhelming.

Besides relinquishing their paychecks every two weeks, halfway house residents must face daily indignities. Each resident must hand over her bag for inspection every time she returns to the halfway house to ensure she is not bringing in contraband such as food, weapons, money, drugs or paraphernalia. The halfway house staff may also check each woman's wallet to ensure she doesn't have too much money. An employed resident is allowed to no more than fifty dollars.

The deadline for getting dinner is 5:30. If a resident's schedule doesn't allow her to arrive on time, she can sign up for a late tray, which is the same food—chicken, overcooked vegetables and mashed potatoes—but cold. After dinner, there are nightly chores, and twice each week there is major cleanup. Job assignments are based on staff preference. Those in poor standing clean the bathrooms.

Every resident of a halfway house works through levels. Working one's levels means that one is moving toward release from the halfway house to parole. There are five levels, each granting increased privileges. Levels help determine who gets which chores and who gets a leisure pass each week to visit her family.

Even if a woman has earned a leisure pass, she is not authorized to visit or otherwise communicate with another felon, even if the felon is a family member. Many of the halfway house residents have family members who also have felony backgrounds, some of whom are in prison. While halfway house residents are allowed to write letters in their free time, they can't write to people in prison. After they achieve the level that allows them to receive leisure passes, the women can visit their kids as long as the kids reside with approved adults. Elaborate shuttling sometimes occurs so that program participants' children are present for a few hours at the home of a particular family member whom the participant is allowed to visit. Women tell me how confusing it can be for their children and how stressful it is to put so much pressure on these visits going well. The purpose of the visits is for the halfway house residents to rebuild relationships with their children, but these stressors make this difficult.

Some women we hire from halfway houses were never in prison. They are referred to as diversion clients. Diversion is an option, in lieu of prison, in which a woman is sentenced to the halfway house. A diversion client must serve her entire sentence in a halfway house, since diversion is the punishment, rather than a transition from prison into the community. She remains at the halfway house until her mandatory release date, or MRD. At the halfway house she is required to participate in counseling, drug treatment and behavior modification classes, just like the other residents. However, diversionary clients do not have to work levels to gain additional privileges. Like other halfway house residents, they must pay for the classes, restitution, and rent. If a diversion participant is successful, her case may be dismissed or she may receive a lesser charge. If she doesn't successfully complete the diversion program, her case will go back to court for prosecution. Often our program participants who were in the halfway house after prison made it clear that they thought women who got diversion instead of prison were suckers.

Samantha's judge wanted to sentence her to diversion instead of prison. The problem was, she'd already entered a plea before going before the judge.

"They were trying to hand me the Big Bitch."

"Excuse me?" I asked.

She smiled, "They were trying to say I was a habitual offender. It was my third offense and they wanted to scare me into rolling on my codefendants. So they were trying to give me time for multiple offenses."

"How much time were they trying to give?" With a name like Big Bitch, I figured it couldn't be good.

"They were talking seventy-two years."

"In prison? Even if you only served half of that time, you'd have been approaching sixty when you got out!" With that sentence, Samantha would spend nearly all of her adult life in prison. What would she have to look forward to?

"I was thinking that too. Then they offered a little bitch—sixteen to twenty-four years. I pled it down to eight to ten years, asking for credit for time served." She already had served six and a half months in the county jail when she was sentenced. She served twenty-eight months in prison before being released to the halfway house. She'd experienced both prison and the halfway house, and thought prison was actually better. At least in prison, she said, it is clear what the rules are.

After years of being told what to do, when and how, by both prison and halfway house staff members, how do any of the women we hire regain their sense of self and personal direction? From where do they gain the confidence that enables them to pull their lives together and succeed? At the Bean Project, we hope that some of this comes from gainful employment.

Fellow halfway house residents aren't likely to provide the support a woman needs. In the evenings, after dinner, residents typically go to their rooms to listen to music or read. They aren't allowed to visit another room; there is to be no appearance that it is a dorm hall. If a resident wants to watch TV, she is required to stay in the TV room. Some residents get portable DVD players as gifts from family members, and borrow movies from the library. But those are women who have begun to work their way up on their levels and receive leisure passes for a trip to the library.

Occasionally someone runs away from the halfway house, taking off rather than returning to the facility at the end of the day. If a runner turns herself in within forty-eight hours, the penalty is typically jail time, usually sixty days. If she doesn't turn herself in, the penalty is influenced by her activities while she is on the run and by where she runs. The district attorney for one county in the Denver metro area pursues an eight year sentence for escape. Eight more years! That's longer than many of the women's original sentences. Typically one is sent back to prison to finish one's sentence, but time served and time already taken off for good behavior still apply. There is an opportunity for additional time off for good behavior. Any additional time for the escape is determined by what she does while on the run, as well as how she is captured. It is not uncommon for a woman to fall into criminal activity while she is escaped. She may relapse—perhaps the reason for the escape in the first place—then she may begin selling drugs, prostituting or performing other illegal activities to support herself and her habit.

Eventually nearly all program participants are placed on Intensive Supervision Parole (ISP), or parole. Parole allows women to move into homes in the community where they complete their sentences. However, the system occasionally sends women directly from prison to parole. If she doesn't have an acceptable home to go to when she's released, she could be "paroled to homeless." Parole can be a confusing and stressful time. There is a whole new set of rules, and the threat of re-incarceration looms ominously for the women. Rather than focusing on their futures, women often are looking over their shoulders for fear they have displeased their parole officers and will lose the ground they have fought so hard to gain.

The disadvantage of this option was driven home when I met with Shelly, the director of a local halfway house. Shelly and I sat in her office on opposite sides of her desk, having a friendly conversation after she'd given me a tour of her facility. I wanted to see for myself the facility that so many of our program participants called home and were working so hard to leave. Shelly's pride in the work done at the halfway house showed in her upright demeanor and confident language. She frequently referred to the women as "residents." She told me about a visit she had made to a parole office.

"I walked into the parole office for a meeting, and one of our former residents was sitting in the waiting room. After her last stay with us, she had returned to prison. She was now being sent directly to parole and was waiting to see her new parole officer. She was sitting in a metal folding chair in her prison sweats—black sweats with a white number on the chest. Next to her on the floor was a clear plastic bag." Shelly used her hands to make a basketball-sized shape. "That was all she had in the world. She got her fifty dollars cash and her motel voucher for a place on Colfax."

Shelly and I both knew Colfax Avenue, the street that runs several miles through Denver and is lined in spots with low-end motels that are well-known for drug activity and prostitution. I wondered how that woman was going to gather herself up and make it. She was going to struggle to get a job—what would she wear to the interview? At least the halfway houses have donated clothes the women can wear if they arrive without any possessions. How was it going to be possible for her to avoid a parole violation and avoid returning to prison?

Parolees live in homes in the community with pre-approved, nonfelon roommates or family, or in apartments by themselves. When a woman in the halfway house earns her eligibility for parole, she appears in front of the parole board and they determine whether she is granted parole. I believe the parole board judges the woman's progress toward long-term sobriety and her overall ability to function in the community with minimal supervision. While there are fewer restrictions during parole, there are still numerous limitations on parolees' freedom, including requirements to stay clean and sober, maintain full-time employment and obey the law. Parolees may not possess guns or have contact with other felons unless prior approval is obtained.

Once parole is granted, women begin the process of finding an apartment, which is inspected and verified before they are allowed to move from the halfway house into their new residence. Parole officers also make unannounced visits to their clients' homes to look for any signs of illegal activity. Many parolees also must wear ankle monitors, devices that send a radio signal at timed intervals that contains location and other information to a receiver. If an offender moves outside of an allowed range, tries to tamper with the monitor, or is not at her residence at the appointed curfew time, the police are notified.

Part of being paroled is meeting with one's parole officer, or PO. After their first meeting with their parole officer, women judge how challenging it will be to work with the parole officer. They hope for someone who is fair, even if they are tough. I never hear stories about sympathetic parole officers. Typically, the relationship between the women and the PO is fear-based. The PO has the power to send a woman back to prison, and the woman spends every day afraid.

When we began selling our products with Walmart.com and were learning their system for ordering, we closely monitored the order management system. When Wal-Mart sent an order, we were notified by email that we had a new purchase order, or PO. Often these orders arrived in the middle of the night, and if several hours elapsed without our acknowledging receipt of the order, we received another email saying we had a "hot" PO. The first time Samantha, our jewelry supervisor, who was also on parole, saw the notice from Wal-Mart, she panicked, trying to figure out what she'd done to make her parole officer angry.

Parole officers require a monthly check-in meeting that is scheduled during work hours. Even when the women arrive on time for their appointments—they know better than to arrive late and make their parole officer mad—the parole officer makes them wait, sometimes as long as two hours.

Mandatory drug tests also must be done during work hours. Women are assigned a color and must call a hotline daily for a recording that says which color is required to appear for a U/A that day. When a woman hears her color, she has until 5 p.m. to appear for her drug test. If she forgets to call and misses the U/A, or misses the drug test for any other reason, such as being unable to leave work, it counts as a "hot" U/A, or positive drug test. She then has to address the issue with her parole officer and deal with the consequences the parole officer deems appropriate.

After release from prison, the halfway house and even sometimes after completing parole, the women continue to pay back their debt to society via restitution. Restitution is the literal payback to society for crimes committed or for the use of public funds, such as foster care for her children, while a woman is in prison.

Stacy was a program graduate who'd been hired as a staff member at the Bean Project when I began working. She was on parole, had regained custody of her two daughters and was paying restitution for back child support and for the fraud she had committed while an addict. She estimated that she might be finished paying back everything she owed after both daughters were fully grown and she was approaching sixty years old.

The monetary obstacles that the women face as they try to pull their lives together after years of addiction, felony convictions and chronic unemployment, cause me to wonder how they stay motivated. Few of them are qualified for high-paying jobs because, in addition to having felony backgrounds, they have low skill and education levels. In 2012, graduates from the Bean Project who moved to a career-entry-level job earned an average wage of $10.50 per hour. Entire industries are off-limits to women with felony convictions, including hospitals, schools and cosmetology. Though prisons offer cosmetology training, a felon isn't allowed to get a license once she is released.

With restitution and the cost of required U/As, counseling and classes, there rarely is much remaining to pay basic living expenses. Money, or lack thereof, is a significant obstacle for the women and continues to be a stressor long after they graduate from the Bean Project. Lack of money limits where women can live, but felons are not allowed to live in Denver Housing Authority homes.

Many women, once they are paroled and have fewer demands and less structured time, struggle to fill their time with productive activities. Often they have few friends. The people they know are usually associated with their former life, and the conditions of their parole prevent them from associating with those individuals. While being paroled is something to celebrate, the women often struggle when it occurs. They don't know how to live alone, they aren't certain how to fill the vast hours of the weekend and they are afraid of their freedom. One program graduate told me, when she was paroled and living in the house her grandparents had passed down to her, that she was afraid to leave her home on weekends because the world moved so quickly, there were constantly decisions to be made and it was scary to have no one telling her what to do.

Unfortunately, these factors tend to pile up on the parolees. A parolee can be returned to prison for committing a crime or violating parole. Most people return to prison for parole violations such as disobeying curfew, a dirty U/A or not attending court-ordered drug classes.

Returns to prison happen frequently. Nationally, 52 percent of former prisoners return to prison within three years of release. Of all the reasons that women I know are sent back to prison, the one that saddens me the most is relapse. It seems we incarcerate people for their addictions, treating the disease with the wrong medicine. If we are trying to prevent a relapse, degrading women by returning them to prison doesn't seem like the solution.

The prison experience creates feelings of powerlessness and

hopelessness that remain after a woman is released. Halfway houses exacerbate those feelings by referring to the women in derogatory terms, and through the restrictions, arbitrary rules and unnecessary inconveniences like spoiled food. Even on parole, the ankle monitor serves as sort of a scarlet letter, ensuring that the public knows the women are felons. I've seen how the corrections system often works against the very change it is trying to create. Rather than being rehabilitated, women become defeated, operating from a place of fear rather than hope for their future.

Restrictions and rules in the corrections system exist to help ensure public safety. Some of the rules make sense. If a woman wants to change her life, she must leave behind many of the people from her past, so restricting a felon's interactions serves a purpose. Allowing felons to earn increasingly greater freedoms by meeting certain requirements, such as attending therapy, staying clean and maintaining employment seems like a good idea; unless the system undermines a woman's success by making it so hard for her to follow the rules. Requiring that a felon pay back their debt to society also sounds like a good idea—except when a woman's wages are garnished to the point that she cannot meet her basic needs and she begins to wonder if working is worthwhile.

The greatest threat to a woman's freedom is loss of her job, yet the system makes it extremely difficult for her to succeed in mainstream employment. Meetings with parole officers are during work hours, and the POs often make the women wait a couple of hours to be seen. If their color comes up on a particular day, women must leave work early to drop a U/A. Court appearances can be another frustration. A woman may take a day off from work for a court date only to wait the entire day and be told she must return the next day — and miss another day of work.

I recommend a balance. Require women to visit their parole officers, but have those meetings during non–work hours. Extend the time to drop a U/A to early evening so she can do it discreetly after work. Insist on repayment of debts to society, but first ensure the women's basic needs are met. Force attendance in treatment classes, but ensure that positive personal empowerment is required as well. Changing the system to be more accommodating and empowering will have a much more positive long-term impact on the women's lives.

CHAPTER 5

THE DEVIL YOU KNOW—WHY DOMESTIC VIOLENCE IS SO HARD TO ESCAPE

I stopped by the shipping department one afternoon after our daily afternoon UPS pickup and talked with Joanna. Joanna was a cute, spunky woman in her fifties with a wide grin and long brassy blond hair. I liked her from the moment she was hired a few months earlier and had noticed other women were drawn to her as well. Often, when she thought no one was looking, I'd noticed, her smile would fade. I didn't know much about Joanna, so I began asking about her background. She was extremely deferential, which made her seem to have very little self-esteem, always answering my questions with a "yes ma'am" or "no ma'am." Her focus on pulling orders accurately, her attention to her work and her ability to learn new tasks led me to wonder about her life before prison, the halfway house and the Bean. She wasn't learning to work. I don't remember exactly how her background came up, but I probably asked her about her family and whether she had children.

Joanna described how one night, as her husband towered over her with rage, she realized that if she was going to live, she had to get out. He must have been extremely intimidating; Joanna was short, barely five feet tall. She described how he had hit her for twenty years. In the early days, when she had young children, she wasn't willing to disrupt their lives. Years later, she didn't have the support she needed to leave. She went to her family many times, but they were not supportive of her leaving her husband, telling her that women are supposed to stay and not disrupt the family. When she finally decided to go, her family abandoned her and refused to give her money or a place to stay, even temporarily. She ended up homeless. Joanna's courage to leave everything—a business she and her husband had built, their children, and her home—resulted in her losing all she had held most dear. Already in her forties, Joanna felt she had little to live for, and began using drugs and hustling to have a place to stay every night.

This was the first story of abuse I heard, but not the last. Over time I have learned to recognize the signs of domestic violence, and, as I've gotten to know the victims, I've developed a better understanding of why abusive relationships can be so hard to leave.

"I was not street smart," Joanna explained. "I didn't know anything about anything and I eventually caught a case."

"Caught a case?" I asked.

"You know, got arrested, charged and, eventually convicted."

"For what?"

"Possession with the intent to distribute. But I wasn't going to distribute. It was all for personal use."

I asked if she was back in touch with her family. Surely, once they saw what had happened, they would support her. She looked to the floor, "No, especially now that I am a felon, they won't have anything to do with me."

I imagined the inner strength Joanna must have had to tap to find the courage leave her husband. I wondered if, in her shoes, I could have done the same. I recalled a relationship I'd had in my late twenties. I was living in Chicago, feeling confident and enjoying the single-career-life in a big city. Then I met Tom. Although I believed myself to be emotionally healthy at the time, feeling secure in my independence and my ability to support myself, this relationship seemed to tap into latent insecurities. I was active at the time, meeting girlfriends for coffee, competing in triathlons and traveling for my job, but what I remember most was turning down invitations—to parties, small social gatherings, Thanksgiving dinner with close friends—because Tom didn't want to go and didn't want me to go by myself.

As the relationship progressed and my confidence eroded, I felt a sense of despair after our frequent arguments. I recall entering into arguments feeling confident that I had a valid point to make, only to feel the tide turn against me in the middle of the disagreement. One evening after work I ordered Chinese takeout for dinner. Tom was scheduled to stop by to share it. He was thirty minutes—then forty-five minutes—late. I called his apartment several times, leaving multiple messages. After an hour, I ate and cleaned up, placing the extra food in the refrigerator. I was angry; mostly because I felt stood up, but hoped there was a good explanation. When I didn't hear from him, I called him mid-morning the next day, again getting his answering machine. Finally, at the end of the day, just as I was leaving my office, my phone rang. It was Tom.

"Stop leaving me messages," he said with no introduction.

"I was concerned when you didn't show. Weren't we supposed to have dinner last night? I ordered enough for both of us."

"I decided I didn't feel like having dinner with you." His words stung. I was uncertain what I'd done that deserved the contempt I heard in his voice, and immediately felt myself panicking. What was going on?

"I'm sorry. What's wrong?" I'm embarrassed to think how I must have sounded back then—desperate, ready to apologize for an unknown failing.

"If you can't figure it out, I'm not going to tell you."

I began to feel angry, frustrated and uncertain as to how I was supposed to guess what could have possibly made him so upset. I explained that I couldn't improve if I didn't know what was bothering him. Besides, how was it that he was upset with me? I had bought dinner and he didn't show. It seemed as though I should have been upset with him. I may have said some of what I was thinking. I remember feeling empowered by defending myself.

My defense set him off and began a pattern of conflict we would eventually repeat over and over again. I could feel him circle like a hunter stalking its prey. He'd search for my weakness and exploit it. Within no time, I'd begin to doubt myself, back down, and try to make amends. Why should he have come over for dinner, he asked? If I didn't have a clue as to why I'd made him so angry, there was no need for him to explain. I owed him an apology. I never did find out why he'd stood me up. The next day he showed up at my apartment as though nothing had happened. When I saw him, I apologized.

Over time, I began to doubt myself and search for all of the ways I had created discord with him. I felt every disagreement was my fault; that his happiness or lack thereof was my responsibility. While sometimes I felt angry and manipulated, overall, my self-image began to erode. The slightest frown or comment from him was enough to make me doubt myself. It was unpredictable and confusing. And when he drank, it was always worse.

It is ironic that Tom tried to control my behavior given that he was so poor at controlling his own. For instance, he was not able to have just one drink; he frequently drank to the point of being sloppy drunk. He started and ceased exercise programs more times than I could count. I was always the disciplined one, the designated driver, the consistent exerciser.

I don't know why I cared so much about his approval. Perhaps his disapproval tapped my need to please or insecurities about my self-worth, or both. Maybe I had an inability to accept failure. If I failed at this relationship, what did it say about me?

One gray Sunday afternoon, about eighteen months into the relationship with Tom, my girlfriend Kelly invited me for coffee. Kelly and I had been close friends since college, and we had helped each other dissect good and bad relationships through the years. I do not remember how she brought it up, but I recall having the sense that she had an agenda.

"What is happening with you and Tom?" she began by asking. That gave me the opening I needed; I began lamenting the minutiae of our disagreements; how he had gotten angry about something I said, how I hadn't realized he didn't like me to speak with a particular girlfriend, always ending the story with "But I realized I probably shouldn't have brought up the topic" or "I felt bad afterward" or some such comment. I remember having a hard time hiding my feelings of despair from Kelly. "I feel like I am trying so hard to make everything be perfect, and I can never win," I told her.

"Tam, I am concerned about what is happening to you in this relationship. You are no longer the confident friend I know." Her words jarred me. Were these feelings of inadequacy and insecurity pervading all of my behavior? Were they that obvious?

Kelly helped me realize that the doubts I had about myself were related to my relationship. She opened the door to allow me to think differently, to believe that maybe I was not always wrong. She encouraged me to admit that this relationship was unhealthy. Yet it still took a few more months for me to gain the confidence to break up with Tom.

Over a long weekend in the middle of the summer, Tom and I went on a camping trip to western Illinois. The trip was a bust. Our tent was cramped, Tom refused to eat the food I brought, and when we went for a bike ride, he broke his chain while trying to muscle up a hill. Less than twenty-four hours into a three-day trip, we bailed and came home. He didn't speak to me the entire two-and-a-half-hour drive. Tom was clearly fuming about something, but I was too afraid to ask. When he dropped me off at my apartment, he unloaded my belongings at the curb and drove off, leaving me to figure out how to walk a half-block and three flights of stairs with more equipment than I could carry in a single trip. I was lucky; a friend walked by and helped. Nearly thirty minutes later, just as I was hauling the last of my belongings into my apartment, my phone rang. It was Tom calling to tell me he'd been thinking about what a waste of money the trip was. He berated me for doing a poor job of planning. He continued by saying he did not know why he was with me, he did not get anything out of it.

I snapped. I don't think we always know what causes us to take action against an abusive person, but for me this was it. As Tom ranted about what a disappointment I was—not the trip, but me—it finally dawned on me: it was statistically impossible that I could be wrong

100 percent of the time. That realization provided the motivation I needed to finally end the relationship during that phone call.

I recognize that it's hard to compare my relationship with Tom to other abusive relationships. We were not married, we had not built a life together, we did not have children. Plus, I could support myself without him. But that relationship gave me insight into how insidious abusive relationships can be. Not all women are as independent and financially stable as I was.

I've met many women at the Bean Project who've been in abusive relationships and I'm always struck by the similarities between their experiences and mine. We all feel that we are at least partly to blame for the abuse, we think the relationship can be fixed and we have trouble ending it because we believe our inability to make the relationship work is a personal failure.

Over time, as I considered my experience and listened to the stories of the women we employ, I began to understand that every woman has her reasons for staying in an abusive relationship, and it's often difficult for people outside that relationship to understand those reasons. My education into the nature of serious physical abuse began with Colleen.

Colleen was a petite woman who hid behind long bangs that swept across one eye. She had "meth mouth"—broken, blackened teeth stumps that were hard to look at without wincing from the pain she must have been experiencing. Colleen was quiet, so it took a while for everyone to get to know her. But as she came out of her shell, she began to develop friendships with her fellow program participants while they sat elbow-to-elbow at the jewelry production table. They all found her easy to be around and appreciated that she was a hard worker.

After working at the Bean Project with perfect attendance for more than three months, Colleen called in sick one day. When she returned the next day, she was wearing a cast around her ankle. She said that she'd tripped and broken it. But her co-workers noticed that whenever she was asked what had happened, she gave a different story. Once she said that she'd tripped, another that her leg was shut in a car door, another that she'd fallen over her dog. Finally, she confessed quietly that she had broken her leg when she jumped out of the second-story window to get away from her husband who was attacking her. Her fellow program participants told me she had come to work before with other injuries: a black eye from "tripping and falling on the coffee table" and a split lip from "running into a door."

Her supervisor, our case manager and I met behind closed doors to discuss possible ways to assist Colleen. Her supervisor and peers began a campaign to convince her to leave her husband. Our case manager worked to find her a bed at a shelter. After that had been arranged, the group attempted to help Colleen make specific plans to leave her husband. She resisted our efforts to help. While her reasons for not leaving varied, they typically centered around the fact that she didn't want to abandon her dog.

I was frustrated with Colleen for not leaving; it was my first experience working with someone in the throes of abuse. Every other abused woman I'd met at work had already left the relationship. I didn't know what to do other than encourage her to leave her husband, ensure she had a place to go, and help her keep her job. The rest was up to her.

Colleen had become good friends with a fellow program participant named Christina who worked with her in jewelry production. Christina knew all about the abuse and volunteered to serve as our conduit to push Colleen to leave her husband. Christina called Colleen every evening and on weekends to check in with her and let her know she was available for moral support. This made Colleen's husband livid. He began calling and stopping by the Bean Project to threaten Colleen and Christina, saying he would kill them both.

No one really knew if he was serious or just threatening, but it changed my perspective on the situation. I had believed that we could help Colleen by directing her to resources such as housing, but that we shouldn't get involved more than that. As soon as Colleen's husband showed up at the Bean Project and began making general threats, the threats were no longer just about Colleen. Because we are a place of employment, it is our responsibility to create a safe and accepting work environment. This man, along with Colleen, if she decided to stay with him, was a threat to everyone's safety.

As CEO, I had a responsibility to the group. I called the non-emergency line of the police department, hoping I could file a complaint that might at least keep him from coming to the Bean Project to threaten the women. However, only the person receiving a direct threat can file a complaint, and neither Colleen nor Christina felt empowered to do so. For a quick moment I contemplated putting myself into a situation where I would have an interaction with Colleen's husband so that he would threaten me, giving me the fodder I needed to file the complaint myself. This seemed extreme since I didn't know how serious he was. Instead, we increased the pressure on Colleen, and even found a home that would take her dog. Her coworkers kept saying, "Do something!" Finally, she did: she quit her job at Women's Bean Project. When she called in to tell her supervisor, she said she couldn't bear to think that someone else might be hurt because of her. None of us heard from Colleen again.

Colleen's situation compelled me to learn more about domestic violence. Why do so many women stay? What is the dynamic that develops in abusive relationships? Another reason women often don't leave abusive relationships is because they cannot afford to. Colleen's husband may have felt threatened by her leaving their home every day and earning her own money. As an additional means of control, a batterer often limits his victim's access to money. She may have to ask him for even small amounts of money. This has the dual benefit to the abuser of keeping tabs on her and making her dependent on him.

Emotional abuse tends to chip away at self-worth and independence — exactly what I experienced. Often, before battering begins, the abuser starts by controlling the victim's life — the way she dresses, with whom she associates, how she speaks. Over time, this often escalates to physical control through battering. Many women feel they are responsible for making relationships work; if the marriage fails, so do they. The abuser makes the woman believe that his control comes from a place of love. He wants her to look good for him, doesn't want her to spend time with others who "bring her down," wants to take care of her — she doesn't need her own money. Some women can't believe their good fortune at meeting someone so generous.

Some women also stay in abusive relationships because they don't have anywhere else to go. In most communities the number of women who require help far exceeds the number of available beds at shelters. By the time a woman contemplates leaving, going to live with family or friends may no longer be an option. Even before physical abuse starts, an abuser tends to isolate his victim by limiting her access to family and friends. It gives him more control — and her less. Once she really needs those connections, the abuser has ensured they are gone.

It's especially difficult for women in small communities to find a safe haven from an abusive relationship. This was Penni's story. Penni was in her early forties when she arrived at the Bean Project one sunny morning to apply for a job. She looked worn out and malnourished, wearing an oversized jacket over a short-sleeve t-shirt and jeans that hung on her slim frame. Her hair was brushed away from her face in a way that accentuated her sad, pale-blue eyes. She'd been referred by a new acquaintance at a nearby homeless shelter where she had arrived only a few of days before on a Greyhound bus from Missouri. She carried all her belongs in a plastic trash bag and didn't know anyone in Denver. She had escaped an abusive marriage a few weeks earlier and moved into a battered women's shelter near her home town. Although the locations of shelters are confidential, her husband discovered her whereabouts and threatened to kill her, the shelter's staff and other residents. It was determined that the only way to keep everyone safe was to put Penni on a bus to a new city where her husband couldn't find her. She arrived on the doorstep of the shelter with nothing, including no work skills. Penni hadn't worked for years; her husband hadn't allowed it.

This highlights another problem. Even if a woman does have family or friends willing to put her up, she may be placing herself and them in danger. Statistics show that a woman is most likely to be killed by her batterer once she finally leaves and he feels a loss of control.

Even Tom didn't let go when I broke it off. He called my friends, asking them to reason with me. He showed up at my apartment and workplace until I became concerned and my friends jokingly dubbed him "the stalker." But I found too much truth in the comment for it to be funny. During one unannounced visit to my office, he asked if we could go to counseling and said, "You know I have always been able to admit it when I was wrong." I actually laughed out loud at that statement. He immediately turned on me, saying, "I don't like who you have become." The old me, when I was with Tom, would have been wounded and would have tried to immediately smooth over the situation. I stayed quiet and realized that I'd already moved to a healthier place.

Many women choose to stay in abusive relationships because leaving the relationship could thrust them into poverty. Certainly this was the case with Joanna. She and her husband had built a financially stable life together, but he controlled the bank accounts. Women sometimes haven't worked outside of the home during abusive marriages, and they struggle to find employment to support themselves and their kids when they leave.

Joanna's family pushed her to stay and work on the marriage. Losing everything and eventually declining into drugs and crime left Joanna without the self-esteem she must have needed leave her husband in the first place. During the time I knew her, she eventually began to re-establish a relationship with her children, but I think the hurt of being abandoned by the rest of her family took a long time to recover from.

Children complicate a woman's choices. Leaving her abusive home means uprooting her children and finding a safe place for them as well, finding a new school and addressing the trauma of breaking up their home. A woman rarely will leave her home without her kids, even though witnessing the violence will have long-term effects on them as well. Research shows that boys who witness domestic violence are likely to commit it as adults.

Sharifa knew it was damaging for her kids to witness the abuse her fiancé, their father, was inflicting on her. By the time she was twenty-one, she'd already been with him for six years and had three children with him. He provided for her and the children with proceeds from his drug dealing. This financial security was hard to give up. Plus, the idea of leaving the abusive relationship felt even more dangerous than staying. She thought that the way to stop the abuse would be to get on equal footing with him—make him as afraid of her as she was of him—so she bought a gun.

Sharifa arrived at the Bean Project when she was sent to the halfway house after serving seven years in prison. She had large, bright eyes, a big smile and an outgoing personality, always engaging others in conversation and laughter. She'd been convicted of involuntary manslaughter and given a twenty-six-year sentence, but had been released after seven years. Sharifa was quick to tell me that her fiancé had been killed during one of their disagreements.

On the night Sharifa killed her fiancé, he had choked her until she passed out. They were in their bedroom, in the apartment they shared, although only Sharifa's name was on the lease. He didn't have an official job, unless you counted dealing drugs. As she regained consciousness, on the floor between the bed and the dresser, her two-year-old daughter was patting her on the face and saying, "Wake up, Mama!" This was not, by far, the first incidence of violence, but this time Sharifa hoped to gain some control of the situation. She had a license for the gun that she pulled out and pointed at him after she came to and shooed her daughter from the room. He was not fazed and merely replied, "Go ahead and shoot me. I don't care." She had no intention of shooting him, and the gun clearly did not intimidate him as she'd hoped. She realized the futility of her actions and threw the gun onto the bed.

That was a mistake. He had no qualms about using the gun against her. When he picked it up, she went for the gun. In the midst of their struggle, the gun went off. A bullet went into his lung and then his heart, killing him instantly. Later, the police were unable to determine who pulled the trigger.

Sharifa might have acted differently if she had known the statistics. Research demonstrates that having a gun in a home where there is domestic abuse makes it twelve times more likely that someone will be killed. But Sharifa did defy the statistics in another way. A study done in 1998 found that for every one woman who used a handgun to kill an intimate acquaintance in self-defense, eighty-three women were murdered by an intimate acquaintance using a handgun.

I found it interesting that she thought brandishing a gun would solve her problem. I'd always heard that a woman is much more likely to be injured or killed by her own gun. But Sharifa was desperate. She'd tried to tell her fiancé's mother about the abuse and was told she probably was doing something to provoke him. Sharifa later confirmed that her fiancé had grown up in an abusive home. When Sharifa told her own mom about the violence, her mother told her to leave him.

But she didn't. Eventually, her entire life revolved around anticipating when he'd hit her again, then recovering and trying to cope with the latest incident. There always was a period of reconciliation after a violent episode. "After the beating, here come the presents," she said.

Sharifa talked about how, after the first time he hit her, it became her fault. After that, she fed into the pattern, enjoying the presents he would give her after the abuse and knowing that it was a form of compensation so she would stay.

Men express guilt—not about the abuse, but about how the victim made him do it, using language like, "If you didn't make me so angry I wouldn't have to hit you." Then, perhaps recognizing what he's done, an abusive man often becomes remorseful, needy and dependent. The woman then feels sorry for him and talks herself into believing that he will not abuse her any more. That's partly why women don't leave right away, if ever. The cycle of violence follows a pattern: abuse, then recovery when the physical wounds heal and the abuser works to make amends; then he begins efforts to regain control. The cycle begins to escalate again when the abuser fantasizes and plans for the next episode of abuse, imagining what she will do that will make him mad. Then he sets up the victim to justify the abuse.

When she finally had enough, Sharifa decided to do something for herself and her children. But in that one act of violence, she threw away her future. She had never been in trouble before, and, when the police arrived on the scene, she told the truth about what had happened. The shooting was not intended, so she felt she had nothing to hide. The prosecutor said that her purchase of the gun indicated there was premeditation. She was charged with first degree murder. After hearing testimony, the jury determined it was involuntary manslaughter. But the judge was not sympathetic, believing she had contributed to the violence, and sentenced her to twenty-six years in prison—an extraordinarily long time for such a conviction. Her children stayed with Sharifa's mother when she went to prison. Sharifa's legal counsel appealed the sentence, and after seven years, the same judge reviewed her case and determined that the original sentence was too harsh. The judge asked her if she had learned her lesson, then released her to community corrections, the halfway house. By then she had to get reacquainted with her children and rebuild her life as a felon.

Fortunately, not all of my experiences with women who have suffered domestic violence have been so sad. Chalina was barely twenty-one when she started working at the Bean Project. Her clear blue eyes implied innocence, but once we heard her story, we knew that innocence had long been lost. During her intake session, she described what sounded like a made-for-TV movie. Sitting across the table from our social worker, she talked about how her mother introduced her to cocaine when she was twelve. When she was thirteen, her parents separated, but her mother, because of her own addictions, saw Chalina as competition for boyfriends and kicked Chalina out of the house. With the streets as her only home, she had to drop out of school. She was not old enough to work, so she wandered with no purpose or responsibility. But she had the drugs, saying, "When I was using I wasn't hungry or tired or scared."

Chalina spent five years abusing drugs and living a life of violence, being threatened, poisoned, robbed, held at gunpoint and even threatening others with guns, all to score and survive. Finally when she was eighteen, the nightmare stopped. She was arrested for manufacturing, with intent to distribute drugs. This was the wake-up call she needed. After she worked her way through the Department of Corrections, her pastor, the one adult she could trust, referred Chalina to Women's Bean Project.

By the time she arrived at the Bean Project, Chalina was accustomed to abuse. While she claimed to be hopeful for her future, she also was reluctant to take responsibility and make changes. During her first few months of employment, her attendance was spotty, and we became frustrated with her. She showed so much potential, but seemed to be throwing away the opportunity for stability and a new life that the Bean Project presented. Perhaps it took time for her to trust us too, but eventually she learned how to open up and ask for help.

One morning she came to work with bruises covering the entire left side of her face, disappearing into her hairline, going around her eye and finishing with an ugly split lip and red, black and blue marks on her chin. She attended the morning meeting and acted as though nothing had happened, as though people arrive to work every day covered with bruises. As we walked out of the meeting, one of her coworkers and I pulled her aside to get the story. She readily told us she had been in a fight with her boyfriend.

"Did he hit you?" I asked.

"Yes, but it wasn't his fault because I went after him first. I shouldn't have done that." Her eyes darted to the corners of the room as we probed to learn the source of the bruises.

My eyes narrowed, "Chalina, it doesn't matter. That's not okay."

For several days, as Chalina's bruises went from red, to purple to black and yellow, she was adamant that she was to blame for the altercation and refused to consider other perspectives. After countless conversations, we were able to help her understand that violence was not safe for either of them and that this pattern—this was not the first time he had hit her—was not healthy. Eventually she relented, and in a teary confession, she said she had to stay with him because she didn't have anywhere else to go. To prove that this wasn't true, we connected her with a community housing resource that helped her find a studio apartment she could afford on her own. The housing gave her the means to leave, but the support system at the Bean Project gave her the courage to follow through.

Upon graduation, Chalina went to work for Safeway as a checker. She'd never known how to count change and she was nervous, but she did it. When she returned after a few weeks, she spoke proudly about her job and her manager, who was very patient. She also enrolled in an adult high school to try to address her third-grade reading level and earn her GED. She was blossoming with newfound confidence.

Many months later, Chalina moved to Wyoming with her brother. We hoped that she could find the stability she had sought for so long. She continued to check in occasionally over the next year, always reporting that she was doing well and, eventually, that she had a new boyfriend who was a really good man.

Then one day Chalina called me. With more enthusiasm than usual in her voice, she said she was moving again, this time with her fiancé. She was returning to Denver briefly to pick up some things she'd left in storage and wanted to arrange a time to stop by the Bean Project—to give us a donation. "I can't afford much," she said, "but I want to say thank you for everything you've done for me." It was the first time in my tenure that a program graduate had returned to make a donation. Chalina invited the staff to her wedding, a small affair in Denver. She was a beautiful bride, no longer the young girl who came to Women's Bean Project, but a woman whose life was entirely different as a result of her time spent with us.

No one understands domestic violence from the outside. It is easy for each of us to think that if we were in an abusive relationship, we would surely leave. It is something entirely different to one day realize that you're in the midst of abuse and try to get out. I know now from countless stories that domestic violence doesn't happen overnight. It occurs bit by bit, scene by scene, blow by blow. Women look up one day with no clear picture of how they arrived where they are, broken down, hopeless and unable to get out.

The first step toward better addressing domestic violence is increased awareness of the cycle of abuse and understanding that it can happen in any socio-economic environment. We must realize that any woman at any age and any income level can be in an abusive relationship. Supportive friends and family who act on signs of abuse — even when a woman denies the abuse by explaining away bruises or making excuses for her abuser — can help. Support organizations, like safe houses, that provide women a safe place to escape and the ability to leave, also are essential.

We all must all have faith in the human instinct for survival, but we must also recognize that the entrapment that an abused woman feels may override this survival instinct. I now have a better understanding of the relentless pressure that confronts a woman in a violent relationship. No situation is straightforward, and it is difficult to fully appreciate how difficult it can be to create a new and safe life. In this country, where women seem to have so much more power than elsewhere in the world, it's shocking that domestic violence and the powerlessness that it creates still exist. Rather than ask why women they stay, the better question may be how we can help more of them develop the courage leave.

The cycle of domestic violence can be stopped, but it requires a multifaceted effort by the community. One way is to engage nonviolent men to provide crisis intervention services and lead support groups for men who use violence. Men who have committed violence can be counseled to speak out against violence and discourage others from adopting abusive behaviors. Children who have witnessed violence should receive support services to help ensure they don't repeat the cycle. Lastly, community members can support the operations of existing safe houses and the development of additional shelters, so that women who need to leave have a place to go.

CHAPTER 6

THERE BUT FOR THE GRACE OF GOD— WHY THE WOMEN ARE THEIR OWN WORST ENEMIES

One day at our morning meeting, Nicole announced, "Ladies, I won't be here tomorrow because I go in front of the parole board. It's in God's hands, but pray for me, please."

All of the program participants understood the importance of the meeting. If parole was granted, she would receive her "out date," or the date when she'd be allowed to leave the halfway house and move into an apartment in the community. One step closer to completing her sentence.

After the meeting, I asked Nicole how she was feeling about the hearing. Did she think she would be granted parole?

She said she wasn't sure, that it was in God's hands.

"Yes, but have you been doing everything you're supposed to so they will grant you parole?"

She said she hoped so, but she still didn't know what they would decide. If it was God's will, she was likely to be granted parole. If not, she wouldn't.

Two days later, when Nicole returned to work, I ran into her while she was placing her purse in her locker. I greeted her with a big smile, expecting to hear good news. Unfortunately, her hearing had not gone well, and parole had been denied. She told me that it was fine, that she realized it wasn't her time, that God had other plans, but I could see the disappointment in her face and the hunch of her shoulders. I asked what she thought she could do differently next time. Did they give a reason for denying her the parole?

"Not really. They just decide. But, it's okay. Next time." She squared her shoulders and took a deep breath.

I could see Nicole had no confidence in her ability to affect the outcome of the parole board's decision—not this one or in the future. This lack of self-efficacy is common with the women I meet at the Bean Project. If the women feel helpless and unable to influence the outcomes in their lives, how are they going to become empowered enough to make the changes that society demands, to successfully finish their sentences, stay out of prison and keep a job? If they rely entirely on external factors, they set themselves up to believe that they have no control over anything that happens in their lives. They are victims of circumstance, of God's will or fate.

As far as I knew, the parole board's decision about whether to grant parole was based on whether Nicole was taking positive steps to change her life such as staying clean, maintaining a job and following the rules of the halfway house. In other words, she was the primary determinant of whether she'd receive parole.

If everything that happens is because of fate, God or luck, then why would anything we do matter? If one believes the world is controlled by outside forces, rather than the other way around, what's the incentive to set goals, change or follow the rules?

We have expressions that imply that we have no control over our destinies. I frequently say that I'd rather be lucky than smart. I believe there is power in putting goals and desires out into the universe, so to speak. The stars align and help things happen that may not otherwise. I once wanted an L-shaped desk in my office, so over the next two weeks, I found a way to mention to everyone I met that I was looking for this particular type of desk. Then, one of our board members brought a friend to the Bean Project for a tour. This friend was consolidating his two companies into one location and shutting down an office. He was trying to get rid of furniture, including two L-shaped desks, if we were willing to pick them up.

In 2008, Women's Bean Project won a contest on HGTV that entitled our building to a complete facelift. Every surface would be painted, the floors refinished, a mural created on one wall. Prior to winning, I proclaimed that if we were selected, I wanted to install an elevator in our two-story building. Everyone asked how I would manage that. The project budget didn't include anything close to the amount needed for an elevator—about $150K. I shrugged and started making calls. Within about a week, I called the right guy on the right day in Denver's Office of Economic Development. He told me that another organization had been forced to give up a grant and, as a result, they had funds to spare. We got a community development block grant from the city for $100,000, giving us the start we needed to raise the rest of the funds from foundations.

I may say that I would rather be lucky than smart, but I also believe that I create my own opportunity. I told people that I was looking for an L-shaped desk. I made the call to the Office of Economic Development. In other words, I created my luck with my actions. My ability to do this reflects a high level of self-efficacy and an internal locus of control. I feel so strongly about my power to affect outcomes that it never occurred to me others don't feel the same level of empowerment.

Self-efficacy is my belief in my own ability to complete tasks and goals. Internal locus of control, a related concept, refers to my belief that I can control the events that affect me. For instance, if a student with an internal locus of control performs poorly on a test, she might attribute her poor performance to a lack of preparation. By contrast, a student with an external locus of control might attribute poor performance to an unfair exam or the teacher's negative feelings toward her. The second student doesn't buy into her ability to control the outcome.

Another expression, "There but for the grace of God go I," puzzled me. I've heard volunteers and donors at the Bean Project say this when asked why they support our organization. One former board member said, "I was wild as a teenager. My life could have easily gone off track." Her point? Without God's intervention, just one bad decision made as a teenager could have led her to be a program participant at the Bean Project rather than a donor and volunteer living in an upper-middle-class suburb with three kids, a husband who was a bank president and a very comfortable life. I suspect she felt some survivor's guilt. Why them and not her?

But was it really God who determined that the board member would dodge negative outcomes, while other women ended up in prison? To explore the topic, I contacted Dean Peter Eaton, the head of St. John's Episcopal Cathedral, where I occasionally attended with my husband and children. I asked the Very Reverend Eaton if he would meet with me to discuss the notion of God's will. I was a little nervous. What if my belief that I control my own destiny put me squarely against the church? He arrived at my office wearing what I presumed were his everyday vestments, a long white robe that fastened at the neck. I could see his khaki pants underneath. The clothes were much more pedestrian than the highly decorated robes he wore on Sundays. I decided to jump right in without an icebreaker and asked, "Does God control our destiny?"

The Very Reverend Eaton, with his polished bald head and equally polished English accent, replied, "This notion that God determines the outcome is false. God is not directing us from above. God has given us the gift of free will." I felt relieved. My gut wasn't so far off from Dean Eaton's perspective.

But program participants don't express this in the same way. When they talk about God, it sounds more like they are ceding control. I know that the idea of a Higher Power is a part of the Twelve-Step Program, and many of our women participate in Alcoholics Anonymous, Narcotics Anonymous and other programs in which the Higher Power is invoked. Is this where it comes from? So many things happen to the women throughout their lives that make them feel as though they don't have control over their destinies. But is giving it all up to God a way to avoid personal responsibility for outcomes? Or does it have to do with feeling helpless? Locus of control falls on a continuum. Someone with a high internal locus of control believes they are responsible for their own success. Someone with high external locus of control believes there are circumstances outside of them, such as luck or God, that determine how things turn out. External locus of control supposes that external forces beyond our control determine our fate. As things around us change, we attribute success or failure to things we control or powers outside of our own influence. An internal locus of control brings the power and control back inside.

Research shows that it generally is more desirable to have a realistic internal locus of control, while also recognizing the influence of others and unforeseen events. Those with high internal control are more likely to work for achievement and tolerate delays in rewards, are better able to resist coercion and are more likely to learn from past experiences. Additionally, they are less prone to risky behaviors and more willing to work on self-improvement and to better themselves through remedial work.

Locus of control develops through life experiences and is associated with family style and resources. Children who grow up in families with a lot of support and positive feedback tend to develop a stronger internal locus of control. High external locus of control is associated with low socioeconomic status, particularly in single-parent families headed by women. While extensive research hasn't been done on the exact determinants of locus of control, it may be shaped by a family's socioeconomic status and resultant parenting styles. Research published by Rosier and Corsaro suggests that parents in lower-income homes tend to stress more authoritarian parenting styles, such as conformity and behavioral rules, while high-income parents emphasize self-direction in their parenting.

In a study conducted by Charles A. Sandoz and published in the Alcoholism Treatment Quarterly, a group of recovering alcoholics in A.A. was compared with a group of non–problem drinkers. Measures of locus of control and emotional maturity were used as points of comparison. The A.A. group differed significantly with the other group in its greater belief in an external locus of control and had greater emotional dependency. A linear relationship was found between length of sobriety and an internal locus of control in the recovering group. That is, being internally focused contributed to long-term success staying sober.

This applies to family members affected by addiction as well. It's easy to imagine how life with an addict could make one feel as though there was no control. The inability to control a loved one's drug use and other behavior easily could be transferred to a belief that one doesn't control any aspect of one's life. Many of the women at the Bean Project grew up with addicts in their homes. It is hardly surprising that they continue to feel little control over their worlds as adults.

These factors make sense, but I worry about women who use their external locus of control to justify unhealthy or unproductive behavior. Upon graduation, Patricia got a job as a teller at a local bank branch that was located on a busy street on the west side of Denver near a number of strip clubs. Patricia became acquainted with the customers from the nearby businesses who came into the bank each morning to make cash deposits. In short order, she saw that the strip clubs were quite lucrative. Over time she became well acquainted with the owner of one of the strip clubs, who asked if she was interested in interviewing to be a topless cocktail waitress at his club. Patricia had a long history of addiction. She had begun stealing alcohol from her father when she was twelve and was an adult alcoholic and intravenous drug user. She had also struggled with eating disorders. When she came to the Bean Project, she estimated she'd been in and out of rehab twenty times. Working at a topless nightclub, where she would be surrounded by alcohol, seemed like a really bad idea, and we told Patricia as much when she arrived to share her good news about her interview. Patricia replied, "If God didn't want me to have this opportunity, He wouldn't have presented it to me." Patricia's belief made her feel better. It was in

God's hands, not hers.

Patricia went to the interview a few days later. She called after the interview to tell us that she had not been hired. She sounded disappointed, but I was glad it didn't work out. At a minimum, I knew that being surrounded by alcohol would likely lead to a relapse.

I had another interaction that led me to believe that an external locus of control can be helpful. One day after morning meeting, I approached Angela, who had said during the meeting, "I pray to God every day and hope that He can help me stay clean and sober." I wanted to understand her beliefs and how they guided her behavior during her recovery. I stood next to Angela while she scooped chocolate-covered espresso beans into plastic sleeves. She practically oozed positivity. As we spoke, she described her own spiritual awakening, "I needed to surrender my will in life. Basically, the world is good, and good and positive outweigh the bad, but you have to give it all up to God."

"Is your recovery up to you or is it up to God?"

"It is all God's plan. You know when you are going the wrong way. That's God inside of you, telling you it's wrong."

"But what about your own role in it? What about free will?" I asked.

"Look, before, shame prevented me from talking to God. What I learned from the Twelve Steps is that the sooner I stop blaming and labeling myself, I can start healing. Today, knowing God is with me gives me strength."

It was hard to argue with Angela's approach. It seemed to be working for her. Her belief in God seemed to equate with hope. She was focused on a better future for herself, even though she had lost everything—her middle-class lifestyle, her husband, her children—

to her meth addiction. She couldn't explain how her slide into addiction had led to a conviction and prison time for possession of methamphetamine with the intent to distribute. Angela was always kind, even in her addiction, and an easy mark for other addicts. She never sold meth but was always willing to give away whatever she had to whoever was willing to take it. Raised in a Southern Baptist family and taught to be kind and generous, it wasn't hard for her to remain generous when she was on the streets. Returning to her core spiritual beliefs seemed to be working well for her. It was hard for me to understand, but I respected her conviction of faith. Hopefully the Bean Project could help her combine that faith with a belief that she also had some control of her own destiny.

I met with Bob, our services director and a social worker, to discuss how this lack of self-efficacy and this external locus of control affected what we teach the women in the program. Together, we thought it would be interesting to conduct our own study with the staff members and program participants to help learn more about how internal versus external locus of control manifested in our own environment and why our views—because Bob and I shared the opinion that our actions control our destiny—were so different from the program participants'. Bob found a survey developed by the psychologist Julian Rotter, which our staff completed during one of our meetings. He subsequently administered the same survey to all program participants. The survey contained twenty-two pairs of statements. We had to choose one statement from each pair based on which one we agreed with the most. Some sample questions:

"Bad luck is what leads to many disappointments in life" versus "Disappointments are usually the result of mistakes you make."

"Teachers treat students fairly and evaluate their performance as objectively as possible" versus "The grades you earn in school have more to do with factors like how much the teacher likes you or your mood on the day of the test."

I wasn't surprised to find that my score, along with that of most of the staff members, showed strong internal locus of control while nearly all of the program participants were at the other end of the continuum, indicating very high external locus of control.

Besides making us more aware, the survey also helped validate work we were already doing. Every Monday in morning meeting, all program participants and staff members set goals for the week. We each must write down at least one personal, one work-related and one long-term goal we'd like to work on that week. We then go around the room, taking turns, allowing each person to read their goals aloud to the group. Personal goals might include "I would like to go for a walk after dinner three times this week." A work-related goal might be "This week I would like to work with my job coach to update my resume." A common long-term goal is getting current on one's rent in order to get out of the halfway house. Setting goals is the first step toward gaining control of one's life. The second part of the process also is essential. Every Friday morning we again share with everyone in the room, but this time each person must say if she accomplished the goals or what she did to work toward them. The rationale is that combining goal setting with attention to how one is making progress toward achieving one's goals makes an even greater impact on the development of internal locus of control.

It is hard to adequately describe the transformation I witness in the women during their tenure at the Bean Project, especially during morning meeting. When women first arrive, they often will not look me in the eye. They appear angry or defensive. Then, little by little, they begin to soften. They begin to smile more. Their goals become more substantial. They go from saying, "My goal is to make it to work every day this week." to "My goal is to get my kids back." The latter goal is much more difficult to achieve, requiring planning, consistency and follow-through. Eventually things that seemed overwhelming and impossible begin to show up on their goal sheets. They dare to dream. Although we don't perform pre- and post-evaluations of locus of control, our morning meetings indicate that the Bean Project has an effect.

Brenda is an inspiring example of the effectiveness of our morning meetings on developing internal locus of control. Before Brenda came to Women's Bean Project, she struggled to move from welfare to work. She didn't have a felony conviction, so she and her family qualified for subsidized housing through Denver Housing Authority. Her husband had a low-paying job and couldn't support their family of five alone. They were receiving assistance, but the benefits were going to expire, so they needed Brenda to get a job and keep it.

Brenda was guarded during her first few weeks. She seldom smiled and she was quiet, while her face wore a constant scowl. She was always neatly dressed with ironed jeans and well-fitted shirts. Little by little, she began to warm up to the group as a whole and to a few of the staff members in particular. Things seemed to be going well for Brenda—she came to work every day and on time—until one morning she was extremely belligerent during morning meeting. At the end of the meeting, another staff member and I pulled her aside and asked what was going on. When everyone had left the room, we sat back down at the tables, one of us on either side of her. She was not immediately willing to share, but finally she said that she had noticed that in two days it was her turn to run morning meeting. Not understanding the problem, I asked, "What does that have to do with how you are acting today?"

"When it is your turn to run morning meeting, you have to read out loud. That's just stupid." It seemed such a strong reaction that I began probing. Was she afraid to speak in front of the group? Did she have issues with other program participants that made her feel uncomfortable? No, Brenda said, it wasn't any of those things. I stayed quiet as Brenda's entire physical demeanor changed. She became agitated and nearly frantic and finally blurted out, "I can't read in front of everyone!"

"You can't read?" I asked as kindly as possible, wondering how, she had gotten past our screening if she was illiterate. Literacy is a requirement for employment at the Bean Project because participants need to read labels, recipes and instructions. "I can read!" she cried defensively, "I just don't want to do it in front of everyone!"

Clearly, there was a problem. Perhaps the easiest solution was to have someone else run morning meeting that day. Then Brenda said something that got my attention.

"Maybe I just won't come to work that day." I knew from Brenda's work history that she had landed many jobs, but never stayed at any one job longer than a few months. Our objective at Women's Bean Project is to help women break such a pattern. I had an idea.

"Brenda, do you know any quotes?"

She said no.

"Okay, how about this? What if you take one of the books we use in morning meeting home with you for the next couple of days and find something you like that is short and memorize it? Then you could come to morning meeting in two days and act as though you are reading, but really you will have memorized it instead. Would that work for you?"

Brenda had been staring at the table, but a few moments after I proposed this solution, she looked up at me with a silly, gap-toothed grin. "Our secret?" she asked.

I still wasn't clear what the problem was, but she had agreed to face her discomfort rather than avoid it as she'd done in past positions.

"Our secret," I promised.

I wasn't entirely certain Brenda would go ahead with the reading, but two days later, she showed up for work on time. She said good morning with a conspiratorial smile in my direction and confidently asked if there were any announcements. After a few announcements about upcoming events for the day, Brenda pulled out the book she had taken home, put on a pair of glasses, removed a bookmark and began to read a quote from the book. I'd have sworn she was reading, that she had not memorized it, but regardless, she pulled it off and no one was the wiser. I was proud that she chose to confront her fear rather than run from it. Interestingly, after that morning she began to wear her glasses constantly — something she'd never done before. This small gesture of taking control made all the difference.

A few weeks later, we were conducting a pre-hire orientation for prospective program participants. We conduct these sessions to let women know what they can expect from the Bean Project if they are hired, as well as to get a sense of what we expect in return in terms of their participation in both the work environment and the program. We find that this pre-hire orientation is a great way to ensure everyone is clear on what we are working to accomplish during the program participants' time working at the Bean Project. An important aspect of this pre-hire orientation is the assistance from current program participants, since they are in a perfect position to speak honestly about what the program requires as well as its benefits. As a way to assess reading ability and provide interaction with the prospects, we ask program participants to help read aloud the handouts that review the policies and expectations of the program. At this meeting, Bob started out by asking for a volunteer. Up shot Brenda's hand. With a smile on her face, she stood up in front of the group and read aloud a paragraph she had never seen before. I was astonished and so happy she had found her reading voice! She was no longer allowing her fear of reading aloud to control her actions. Maybe only Brenda and I knew the significance of this accomplishment; at the break, I gave her a knowing smile, and we hugged.

Julian Rotter said humans can interpret all events as either being a result of one's actions or coming from external factors. Whether you believe you can control a situation will determine your reward expectations and behavior. Though internal versus external locus of control focus can vary based on circumstances, Rotter said people generally trend toward one or the other according to their personalities and life experiences.

If locus-of-control beliefs are not genetic, but environmental, it follows that these attitudes can be changed. In a study conducted by the Urban Institute, prisoners were asked about their readiness for change, self-esteem and control over life. Most respondents, released prisoners with felony convictions who were working to reenter their communities, had a strong desire to change their future behavior. Ninety-seven percent said they wanted to get their lives straightened out. Nearly two-thirds had strong feelings of control over their lives just before they were released from prison. Subsequently, a locus-of-control scale, developed specifically for prisoners, found that inmates who are more internally focused adapt better to prison life. Ultimately, these released prisoners also had lower recidivism.

How can we help the women in our program perceive that they have some control over their lives? This is a particularly difficult challenge given the inherent restrictions and external controls imposed by halfway houses, drug tests, parole officers and financial-restitution requirements. Each day so many of our employees respond to external forces such as the criminal justice system or prejudices from prospective employers.

When I meet the women, they are at the mercy of the criminal justice system and other outside forces. Granted, many of these constraints are consequences of their own making. And, while a victim mentality can easily lurk round the corner waiting to take charge, I've seen that the women who do best in our program are those who understand their role in their success. Sure, they may not know when the next U/A will be required, but they can choose not to use drugs so that the timing of the test doesn't matter. They can't change how society views them and their felony record, but they have the ability to work toward finding a job at a felon-friendly employer where their skills and talents can shine. They can't predict when someone from their past may return to pull them off track, but they can choose not to get sucked in.

Maybe it's easy for me to believe that I control my destiny. I am the primary actor in my life and the consequences of my actions are largely positive. But even though my day-to-day choices and decisions are different from the program participants', each time I make a choice toward a larger goal, I manifest my own internal locus of control. Even when luck is present, I help to ensure that the proper set of circumstances exists so that I'm poised, ready to snatch the luck as it whizzes by.

Women's Bean Project is about second chances. Women arrive on our threshold barely able to dream. A big part of our job is to ensure they don't feel resigned to a particular fate. Though the women arrive with few options, their job is to take control. They must not cease trying to achieve their goals. If nothing else, their peers in the program won't allow it. The dynamic that occurs in morning meetings precludes anyone from keeping their dreams secret or ignoring their commitment to accomplish a life change.

If our locus of control is not genetically determined but is instead a belief system, then it can be changed. Perhaps the first step is to change from "I can't help it" to "I can help it." I believe the Bean Project can assist with that. Believing in another person can have powerful, life-changing results. When we believe in someone, she can finally begin to believe in herself.

CHAPTER 7

CHICKENS AND EGGS—HOW MENTAL ILLNESS, DRUG USE AND POVERTY INTERSECT

Crystal grew up in poverty and surrounded by addiction. Her parents were meth addicts who split when she was barely a year old. After her parents' breakup, her mother developed a propensity for abusive relationships. Crystal watched her mom abuse meth for years before she tried it at age thirteen. So began ten years of meth use, during which Crystal developed the habit of trying to stay awake for as long as two weeks at a time. Fueled by meth and a youthful exuberance, she thought that it would be cool to see how long she could go without sleep.

At twenty-three, Crystal's world changed significantly when, as she describes it, "she got a demon." Crystal's demon was mischievous; it opened and closed doors, prevented her from opening a bible she held in her lap, tried to talk her into hurting other people. After a few weeks of experiencing her demon, Crystal determined that if the demon was real, then God was real and she needed to get clean. She turned herself into the police, was arrested for possession of meth and received a diversion sentence to a halfway house. Crystal had been clean for nearly a year before she worked at the Bean Project, but she still believed strongly in her demon. When she was released from the halfway house and moved into housing designed for recovering addicts, she was nervous about living alone, afraid because she believed her demon would return if she lived by herself.

Most likely, Crystal's demon was caused by psychosis generated by her prolonged meth use. The Meth Project describes psychosis caused by meth as a severe mental disorder in which people lose contact with reality and experience strong delusions, extreme paranoia, hallucinations and obsessive-compulsive behavior. Many of the women at the Bean Project start to abuse drugs during adolescence. Drug use during a teenager's formative years can interfere with normal socialization and cognitive development, which then can lead to mental disorders. At the Bean, I've met numerous women who became addicted to drugs as teenagers, but they typically aren't diagnosed with mental illness until they are adults. It's hard to know which comes first: are these women motivated to self-medicate by a mental illness they don't understand? Or, is peer pressure or a desire to experiment what led to their drug use?

The unfortunate reality is that a high percentage of people with mental illness also are addicted to drugs. Because addiction and mental illness are both brain diseases, it can be difficult to discern which came first. Do drugs cause mental illness or does mental illness lead to drug use? Regardless, both need to be treated. Unfortunately, mental health service providers often are not equipped to deal with co-occurring conditions, nor are drug treatment programs adept at dealing with mental illness. Patients, including our program participants, often get caught in a netherworld in which they are unable to get treatment for either their addiction issues or their mental illness.

I'm not sure which came first for Wanda, a psychological disorder or drug use. Wanda was always positive and upbeat, and frequently caused everyone around to crack up with laughter—including me. A mother of four, she confessed to using drugs off and on since she was young, although she was vague about which drugs she'd used and exactly when she started. She had very unusual verbal tics. Whenever she spoke, she'd punctuate the end of a sentence with a noise, like "Bing!" or "Pop!" or "Zappa whappa do!" Her audience always laughed, as much out of surprise as anything, and Wanda would laugh too. In many ways, the spontaneity of her tics was both delightful and extremely odd. These tics, and her general demeanor, were off-kilter enough that we took her for drug testing more than once. She was always clean.

I was working in the kitchen with Wanda one day, preparing lunch for a tour we were giving at noon. Several program participants had called in sick that day, so I'd gone to the kitchen to help make sure we were ready. Wanda and I initially divvied up the work. At least I thought we had. Physically, Wanda appeared focused, attending to each task, cutting an onion, or stirring the pot of chili, but every task seemed to require more concentration that she was able to muster. To get a sense of where her challenges might lie, I began talking, trying to engage her in light banter. Wanda pleasantly answered my questions, but she'd end every response with quick statements in which she'd repeat the last part of my sentence and then add her signature exclamatory punctuation.

"How's it going over there with the onion, Wanda? I'll need to add it to the chili soon."

"Yep, slicing the onion now. Yamma bing jing!"

"Would you mind stirring this pot while I crack the eggs?"

"Stirring away. Gabba do woo. Bip!"

Between these exchanges about the food preparation, I asked her general questions about her kids, her plans for the future, even the weather. Regardless of what we discussed, Wanda's brain pinballed all over the place, from sentence to partial sentence, interspersed with platitudes like, "I wore welfare into the ground because it was there. It's time for me to pull myself up by my bootstraps and move on down the road." It was both entertaining and exhausting to try to follow along. When I laughed out loud, Wanda laughed right along.

As we worked, I tried to visualize what was going on in her brain. I could only picture popcorn; noisy, active and quick. When we were finished, I sought out Bob, our services director, and told him, "Boy, she must have used a lot of drugs." We agreed her brain didn't function like others' did. Maybe it never had. Wanda came to work every day and eventually graduated the program, but I could see she'd need a special workplace to accept her quirks.

Which occurs first—drug use or mental illness? It depends. Many chronic drug abusers have co-occurring mental illness and self-medicate to alleviate symptoms. In other cases, mental disorders are caused by drug abuse. There is evidence that ecstasy produces long-term deficits in serotonin in the brain, and such deficits are known to lead to depression and anxiety. Meth can trigger latent schizophrenia by sensitizing the brain to dopamine, a brain neurotransmitter. Dopamine is involved in motivation, pleasure and reward, and is also thought to be associated with mental illness.

Drug use as a cause of mental illness is not always entirely clear. More often, there is an interplay between poverty, mental illness and drug use that creates a curious chicken and egg question. Researchers wonder if those with mental illness are more likely to use illicit drugs to self-medicate, or whether drug use triggers mental illness. Which does come first?

Another relationship that's difficult to understand is the link between mental illness and poverty. The World Health Organization, in a 1995 report called *In Bridging the Gaps*, said extreme poverty is the most ruthless killer and greatest cause of suffering on earth. A woman living in poverty is unable to satisfy her own and her family's basic needs. She cannot control her resources and typically is not educated enough to improve her prospects. She has poor general health and a high incidence of psychological problems.

The Bean Project occasionally works with the Colorado Department of Vocational Rehabilitation to offer additional job-training resources to employees. One year, Voc Rehab professionals interviewed all thirty of the women we'd hired. These women had met the Bean's usual criteria of being chronically unemployed and impoverished. The Voc Rehab intake evaluations revealed that 90 percent of our program participants qualified as having a disability, with mental illness—typically depression and bipolar disorder— the most common.

Although the high rate of mental illness was initially shocking, the more I looked into it, the more it made sense. Studies have confirmed that those living in poverty are exposed to more stress with fewer resources to manage the stressors. So they are more vulnerable to the side effects of ongoing stress. There is, in fact, a direct relationship between the experiences of poverty and mental disturbances. The overwhelming majority of people with mental and psychosocial disabilities live in poverty. Christopher Hudson, a researcher at Salem State College, found a significant inverse relationship between poverty and mental illness; that is, individuals with lower socioeconomic status experienced significantly higher rates of mental illness that couldn't be accounted for by other factors. Chronic unemployment leads a woman to poverty, and there is a direct correlation between unemployment and depression, anxiety and phobia. Why this happens is unclear. People who live in long-term poverty may lack the motivation or confidence to succeed, which leads to depression and suicidal thoughts. Or, possibly, mental illness helps put people into poverty because they are unable to hold down a job or manage finances. Regardless, by virtue of the fact that the Bean Project hires chronically unemployed and impoverished women, many have mental illness.

When you pile on lack of access to essential mental health care and medication, poor nutrition and low education levels—all typical for those living in poverty—it is not hard to imagine how the treadmill of poverty can deplete one's energy, increase stress and result in mental illness.

But maybe mental illness causes poverty instead of the other way around? Perhaps people become poor because they've lost their job as a result of mental illness. It seems logical that people with mental illness might live in poverty and that the mental illness came first, causing them to lose a job and drift downward socioeconomically. However, the phenomenon called economic drift, or sliding down the socioeconomic scale as a consequence of mental illness, is rare. The reverse is true. Someone with mental illness is unlikely to move out of poverty. A mentally ill woman is at high risk for staying poor because she is unable to take advantage of opportunities that might move her out of poverty. The cyclicality of the problem is undeniable. How do you keep a job if you're unable to get out of bed each morning? How do you get out of bed each morning if you don't have access to stabilizing medication? How do you afford medication if you don't have an income and health care coverage?

When she was feeling good, Waseme had a sweet, bubbly personality and an engaging tilt to her head when she smiled. On the day she graduated from Women's Bean Project, she wore the royal blue graduation gown with a white t-shirt underneath; her corn-row braids were pulled back into a pile at the back of her head. It was clear that day that she was feeling good. She had been receiving medical treatment for depression and post-traumatic stress disorder for several months.

This image of Waseme on graduation day is so clear in my mind because it stands in stark contrast to Waseme before she got health care coverage, through the Colorado Indigent Care Program (CICP), that provided treatment for depression and PTSD caused by physical and sexual assaults, and enabled her to come to work every day. In the early days of her tenure at the Bean Project, there were days when Waseme called in sick because she couldn't get out of bed. I answered her call one morning and didn't recognize her voice. Instead of the energy I was accustomed to when Waseme came to work on her good days, I heard a gravelly voice that sounded as though, without some lubrication, it might come to a stop.

Even as a lay person, it was easy for me to hear that she was depressed and struggling to manage the ups and downs in her mood. Maybe it was the contrast between when she felt good and when she didn't that struck a chord, but Waseme was hardly unique in her emotional challenges. Depression is defined as despondency that is accompanied by feelings of hopelessness and dejection. Nearly every woman hired at the Bean Project has symptoms of depression.

So if poverty can cause mental illness, does mental illness cause drug use? The likely answer is yes. When a woman doesn't have access to medication to address her mental illness, she is at risk of self-medicating to relieve her symptoms. The hypothesis behind self-medication is that one's drug of choice is not coincidental. Instead, it is the result of the user's psychological condition. For instance, sufferers of depression often choose alcohol, tobacco, cocaine or amphetamines because the effects of these drugs relieve the user's specific condition. Using psychoactive and recreational drugs to alleviate mental illness or psychological trauma provides immediate temporary relief, but self-medicating over a long period has been known to worsen the symptoms of anxiety or depression.

Tania had long been an illicit drug abuser, with cocaine her drug of choice. When she arrived at the Bean Project, she had about one month remaining in her stay at the halfway house, where she'd lived since completing a prison sentence for criminal trespass. When she moved out of the halfway house, she lived with her mother, who was a significant part of her support system. We helped Tania enroll in health care coverage through CICP so that she could get access to treatment for severe anxiety and depression. In addition to these mental health issues, she had many health problems related to injuries: a torn rotator cuff in her shoulder, a bad knee she'd had surgically repaired and an injured wrist from repetitive motion that required a brace.

Tania took a lot of pride in her appearance, and was always very friendly, going out of her way to greet me every morning or stop to talk when I walked past on the production floor. I sometimes was taken aback because she occasionally looked at me with heavy lids and spoke with a slur. Oddly, the next day she usually was fine.

This pattern, one day fine, the next day high, was disconcerting enough that I finally spoke with Pat, our case manager. Pat had been a social worker for a long time and I suspect there was little she hadn't experienced firsthand. She wore a war-weary expression at all times.

"Pat, have you noticed Tania? It seems like she is having a hard time getting her medication dialed in correctly."

Pat sighed, "It's more complicated than that."

I took this to mean she had spoken with Tania's psychiatrist and knew more about the story, but that wasn't the case.

"Tania is a drug abuser. Whether it is street drugs or prescription medication, she manipulates her dosage, mixes medications together and starts and stops medications based on how she feels each day. This is a behavioral problem." Pat went on to explain that although she had tried to help, there was little else she could do. Tania was determined to self-medicate her anxiety and depression in an attempt to make herself feel better. Tania's medical team needed to intervene, and Tania needed to take responsibility for her drug use. Pat said she had urged her, but the rest was up to Tania.

For a while, things seemed to get better. Tania's drug-fog days seemed less frequent. Then one morning we received a call from Tania's family. Tania had died from an overdose of her prescription drugs the previous night. I don't think Tania intended to do this; she may not have realized the dangerous mix of drugs she was ingesting. I was saddened by the news because, perhaps for the first time in Tania's life, she had people trying to help her. But the mental illness and substance abuse were too entrenched.

It's not hard to imagine why a woman living in poverty and struggling with mental illness begins to self-medicate with illicit drugs. She may not have access to insurance, affordable health care and anti-depression medication, but she certainly can gain access—via prostitution, illegal drug sales, or both—to a number of other drugs that will help her feel better—even temporarily—such as marijuana, alcohol or cocaine.

Illicit drug use often leads to the next problem—incarceration. At least 80 percent of the female inmate population have at least one mental disorder, the most frequent being drug or alcohol dependence. A third have PTSD, and nearly 17 percent are diagnosed with major depressive disorder. Years ago, when I first started working at the Bean, the program committee and staff reviewed our criteria for selecting program participants. We asked ourselves whom we could best serve and who would be most likely to successfully complete the program and go on to maintain long-term employment. We came to the conclusion that we were not equipped to address the needs of a woman with mental illness who is not medically stable. Our rationale made sense at the time. The program committee—social workers and mental health and human resource professionals—sat around the conference table and spoke in theoretical terms about the symptoms of mental illness and the impact of untreated psychosis. The extreme cases were easy to imagine. The Bean Project is a chaotic environment, and the committee agreed that such a setting would be unhealthy for mentally unstable women and that, if there was a problem, our staff would be ill-equipped to handle it.

At the time, I didn't know enough to imagine the more subtle manifestations of mental illness, such as those I later saw in Crystal, Wanda, Waseme, and Tania. These women—and many, many more—qualify for our program because their mental illness is not the blatant, severe type we imagined in our planning. It isn't possible to turn these women away; there are too many of them. Instead we have to focus on doing what we can, ensuring that they get health care coverage and helping them access resources such as affordable housing and child care so that the stressors of poverty can be addressed.

One of the greatest difficulties we face at the Bean Project is the complex interplay between mental illness, poverty and drug abuse. We must find a way to address all three challenges if we expect the women to maintain long term employment. The Bean Project's role is to provide a safe and accepting work environment where a woman can develop a foundation for her future while we also help the women gain access to affordable medical care, acquire subsidies for affordable housing, and enroll in programs that provide safe places where their children are well cared for. We will always have program participants with mental illness, but we can build a program that helps them as much as possible. The rest is up to them.

CHAPTER 8

FIRST COMES BABY—
WHY MOTHERHOOD IS NEARLY
IMPOSSIBLE TO AVOID

First comes love, then comes marriage, then comes the baby in the baby carriage. This simple rhyme dictated my view of the order in which my life events were supposed to occur. It was the dogma I grew up with and that guided my attitude, opinions and actions from adolescence through adulthood. In my world, no one wanted to be that girl, the girl who got pregnant and dropped out of school. I shudder to think of the messages I heard in junior high and high school about the loose girls who got pregnant as teenagers. When I was in eighth grade, there was one. Her name was Cynthia and she left school suddenly, causing everyone to wonder. Then one day rumors that she had left to have a baby began to circulate. We all were shocked and confused that someone our age was sexually active and pregnant and that we'd never noticed. I don't know how much of what I heard at that time was true, but fear of being like Cynthia was enough to keep me from having sex.

Into adulthood I believed that girls who had babies when they were teenagers didn't follow the rules and ruined their lives. Then, they made matters worse by dropping out of school. With no skills or education, how were they supposed to get and keep a job and take care of their children? I felt angry at the women who chose to have kids in their teenage years when, in my opinion, motherhood could have easily been avoided. I was sad for their children who had no choice about being born to a teenage mom who likely didn't have the resources to care for them. I worried for the kids' futures, influenced by their teenage mother's poor choices. Until I arrived at the Bean Project, it hadn't occurred to me that the social norms for motherhood vary by community and socioeconomic status, that the dogma I embraced wasn't universal.

I was forty years old and working at the Bean Project when I became pregnant with my daughter. Within my circle of friends and acquaintances it wasn't unheard of for a woman over forty to have a child, but I was certainly on the older end of the spectrum. My husband and I were married when we were thirty-eight, so our delayed parenthood was related to our age when we married. Besides making jokes about using a walker to escort our daughter down the aisle at her wedding, we were comfortable with the timing of our parenthood. It was not part of my life plan to get married and have my first child in my forties, but I had spent the years since college and graduate school in a career-focused frenzy. I had the opportunity to see the world and improve my Spanish-speaking skills while being unencumbered by the responsibilities of marriage and children. One-by-one, my friends got married and started their families. While I traveled to Asia, Europe and Latin America for work and pleasure, I saw their lives as ones of obligation.

Like many women I knew, having children was something I wanted to do someday, but I did not feel any particular hurry. In an abstract way, I imagined meeting someone who I could share my life with, getting married and having one or two children— someday. And while I knew this eventually would require my active involvement, I did not spend a lot of time thinking about it, unless it was pondering about whether the person I was dating at that moment was the right guy. I was not unusual for my demographic. The year my daughter was born, 71 percent of women with newborns were over thirty-five and had at least some college.

When I turned thirty-five, my ability to have children seemed like the only thing anyone wanted to talk about. My physicians reminded me that I was getting older and cited statistics about forty-year-old women's fertility dropping from an average rate of 25 percent to 15 percent. Every time I turned around, someone would remind me that I was not getting any younger. I suppose I should have seen it coming, but I'd been otherwise occupied. I thought about all of the years I'd spent trying not to get pregnant. It seemed ironic that when I finally decided I wanted to have children, I might have difficulty.

At the Bean Project, as with women everywhere, fertility is a common topic of conversation. In every group of program participants, at least one becomes pregnant while in the program. One day, while I was in one of the bathroom stalls, I overheard the following conversation between two program participants who were in their late twenties:

"Oh God, I hope I'm not pregnant. My sister is going to be so mad at me if I'm pregnant again."

"Why will she be mad?"

"Because this would be my second baby and she hasn't had any!"

"Well, why don't you just give it to her?"

I was shocked by the cavalier attitude. They could have just as well been discussing giving away a shirt that was too small.

Regardless of whether I was ready for kids, it was hard to watch program participants get pregnant, usually not for the first time, while they were living in a halfway house or trying to get their lives back together. I wondered how it was logistically possible to get pregnant with the restrictions foisted upon them by the halfway houses and why they didn't use birth control until they were more stable. Adding to my judgment was the fact that most of these women had dropped out of school with the birth of their first child.

Once again I assumed that the program participants should share my values: finish school, get a job, get married, have children. What I didn't recognize is that this is the order in which things happen for women like me who have opportunity. Middle- and upper-class women view motherhood from the standpoint of what they can offer their child. Putting off motherhood for education and marriage helps to ensure the best opportunities for their offspring. Middle- and upper-class women's mindset is to avoid limiting their prospects by having a child too early.

I began researching what motivates poor women like those at the Bean to have kids. Poor women often believe that motherhood provides the most important social role they'll ever have. A woman living in poverty doesn't have power. There are few expectations for educational achievement. Often no one is pushing her to stay in school, and the idea of going to college often is elusive. She has limited economic opportunity and typically doesn't have any role models of women in her community with well-paying jobs. Children provide a tangible source of meaning, a way to gain social status and personal satisfaction. For a poor woman, having a child may be the best that life has to offer. Many poor women perceive a relatively low cost of child rearing and a high value in motherhood.

I know from experience that motherhood brings meaning to one's life, but I believe that it is even more so for poor women who have little else. When I was pregnant I got a glimpse of how a woman's status rises when she is about to become a mother. I was treated differently when I was pregnant. I was special, awarded incessant positive attention, including questions about my overall well-being and the pregnancy. Strangers also smiled at me and offered help whether I needed it or not. While I've never been attention-starved, I basked in this new status: mommy-to-be. It felt good—a warm, snuggly blanket of approval. If I, someone who was generally well-adjusted and happy with myself, liked this attention, I can only imagine how this special status must feel to women in poverty.

Becoming pregnant gave me the opportunity to realize the common bond shared by mothers. I had something in common with nearly every woman we hired. It was an equalizer I had not expected. Our program participants, many of them mothers for years, were in a position to give me advice rather than the other way around. I felt a camaraderie with the women I'd never before felt.

Around the time I became pregnant, we hired a woman named Ronda who shortly after starting at the Bean discovered that she was pregnant with twins. One hot summer day near the end of lunch break, Ronda and I began talking about how we were feeling. She was due in October, and since she was having twins, she already had begun to feel uncomfortable.

"You must have other children," Ronda said to me as we stood by the microwave, warming up our leftovers. Mine was homemade lasagna. Hers was from the local Chinese-food-by-the-scoop place.

"No, this is my first," I confirmed. "How about you? Have you had any other kids?" I was expecting her to say yes, that she had other children. I suspected she was in her mid-to-late twenties.

"No, this pregnancy is my first, but you would think I had committed some crime by waiting so long," she laughed.

"What do you mean that you waited so long? How old are you?" I wondered if I could have misjudged her age by so many years. Was she really close to my age?

"Oh, I'm twenty-six, but since I was about sixteen everyone has been asking when I was gonna have kids. By the time I was twenty they were saying I had to be careful or I'd get too old to have a baby."

I smiled at the irony. "That's funny. People have been saying the same thing to me for years."

"How old are you?" She seemed reluctant to ask, as though she was not entitled to such information about the CEO. When I told her that I was forty, and would forty-one by the time my daughter was born, her eyes grew large. "I can't imagine that!"

"Yes, I guess I have been busy doing other things," I replied, somewhat lamely.

Ronda shared that she, too, had been busy doing other things. She'd grown up in East Denver in a middle-class family in which her mom and dad owned a business. When the business failed they had to sell their house and move to a lower-income neighborhood. Her parents split up when she was eleven, leaving Ronda and her older brother and sister with their mom. Shortly after that, her brother got involved in gangs and, at seventeen, her sister got pregnant. But the sister was not willing or responsible enough to be a mother so, at thirteen, Ronda found herself raising her newborn nephew.

Compounding Ronda's problems was that her mom was using drugs during this time. Ronda protected her mother by not telling her dad that the money he was giving his ex-wife was spent on drugs. But they were living hand-to-mouth, without electricity or telephone service for months at a time. Also adding to the stress was Ronda's mother's abusive boyfriend. She spent many nights listening to her mother's screams and pleas for help.

Not surprisingly, Ronda stopped going to school to stay home and take care of her nephew and mother. She became resentful of her situation as she watched friends go to the skating rink and the park. She felt taking care of her nephew was the right thing to do, but it increased her resolve to avoid motherhood. Just before her fourteenth birthday, Ronda realized that her mother was using her to get her father's money, so she moved to her father's home.

From Ronda's perspective, there were good things and bad things about being with her father. He provided the structure she had not had for several years, but he also provided a strict and demanding environment that caused Ronda to rebel.

"I just manipulated people. I never went to school but still passed my classes. I was messing around and I drank, but I stayed away from drugs. I was a fast-tailed girl."

"What does that mean, fast-tailed?" I asked.

"My lifestyle was pretty much provided by whoever I was dating at that time. They were mostly drug dealers and abusers with nice cars and fast money."

"Did you graduate from high school? It seems like that would have been hard to do." I knew that Denver Public Schools had just a 50 percent graduation rate, so I was expecting her to say no.

Ronda chuckled, "Barely. After that all I did was work and party."

Ronda moved out of her father's house when she was twenty and stayed first with her sister and then with her mom. She hung out with her brother's gangster friends. Her mother was still in an abusive relationship and abusing drugs and alcohol and, according to Ronda, blamed her children for her addictions. By the time Ronda was twenty-one, she was living in a crack house, selling drugs all day and walking the city streets at night.

"Is that what happened? You were arrested for selling crack?" I knew Ronda had a felony background, so this seemed the most likely scenario. It turned out not to be the case at all. She described an elaborate scenario in which she was driving the getaway car for her friends who had shoplifted from a department store. A police officer stopped her, but when her foot slipped from the brake and the car moved, he shot her. The bullet went through her forearm. Once again, I sat across the table from someone who seemed entirely incapable of the crimes for which she was charged, someone who was about to become a mother of two.

"I was charged with eight felony counts, from theft to assault on a police officer."

"You said that you had just gotten out of jail when you came here. You didn't go to prison?" Theft and assault on a police officer sounded pretty serious.

"Well, I couldn't afford a lawyer to fight the charges or sue the police for shooting me. I had to take a deal of second-degree assault on a police officer and misdemeanor theft. I ended up serving 107 days in jail. I got three years' probation plus 100 hours of community service."

"That actually sounds like a pretty good deal, given the situation," I said.

"When I got out of jail nobody would even consider hiring me.

It is hard enough to find a job with a felony on your record, but a charge of assault on a police officer basically made it impossible. Plus, I had nine surgeries on my arm to repair it from the bullet hole." She pulled up her sleeve to reveal the extensive scars. Here was another woman whom the Women's Bean Project was giving a second chance when no one else would, but what mattered most to me was what she would do with that opportunity and how that would affect her twins.

"So now you have this background. No one would hire you when you got out of prison. Do you worry about supporting your kids?"

"No." Ronda shook her head vigorously. "Because of being here, I see that working hard is the best way to support my family." Ronda went on to explain that she was glad she'd waited until she was older to become pregnant. Though she wasn't proud of how she'd spent the prior several years, she knew she was smart to avoid pregnancy during that time, despite the peer pressure she'd received. She wouldn't have been a good mother if she'd begun having kids when she was seventeen, like her sister, she said. Now she was ready to create a life for herself and her twins. Though she didn't say it directly, I could see in her proud behavior and demeanor that, despite the fact that she was building a new life as a felon, becoming a mother would give her life new meaning.

If my prospects for attaining a comfortable life hadn't been so rosy, if I'd had little or no access to an academic degree, a career and a marriage to someone who shared these opportunities, perhaps I wouldn't have been so inclined to put off motherhood for so long. If the only way I believed I could show my value in my community was to have a child and demonstrate that I was a good mother, then why would I avoid motherhood?

Promises I Can Keep is a book about a multiyear research project involving interviews with several hundred women in poor neighborhoods in the Philadelphia area. A common theme among the teenage mothers was the notion that if no one loves you and if you don't have friends, a baby can be your companion and provide fulfillment. I frequently observe this mindset among our program participants. Most are isolated from the support of their family and have limited networks of support. When they announce to the group they're pregnant, I see pride, not fear.

Within my social circles we often talk about being ready to give the baby what it needs. Do we have enough money saved? Do we have a home with the right amount of space? Do we live in a neighborhood with good schools? The poor women I meet think more about what the child can give them: a sense of purpose, a reputation for being a good mother, unconditional love. Having a baby is something that a girl can do to show her value, to achieve something and even be good at. Showing that she can provide food and diapers and keep her child clean is one way that a poor woman can improve her status.

I used to believe that women in poverty had babies to qualify for more welfare benefits or to keep the guy they were "talking to" (which I've since learned means "sleeping with") interested. Like Ronda, many young women in poverty grew up with violence and turmoil and have a strong desire to love and be loved. Kids provide motivation and purpose, though it sometimes may take a woman some time to realize this.

My brother-in-law, Dave, once told me of an experience he had while on the board of the Spot, an evening drop-in center for teens. The Spot is a haven for kids in a safe setting that provides strong peer support and social outlets. The staff and the board were concerned about how many of the girls were getting pregnant. The staff thought perhaps they were contributing to the problem by giving the girls and their babies so much positive attention when they visited the center. It is human nature, isn't it? We're all attracted to babies. The board discussed creating policy mandating that no special attention be paid to a young mother. They would treat her respectfully, but not fawn over the baby when the teen came into the center. The board never instituted the policy, but the notion that seeing girls with babies getting positive attention might lead more girls to have babies has merit.

I used to believe that the poor women who ultimately ended up at Women's Bean Project had children when they were teens because they were either unable to afford birth control or were unwilling to use it for moral or cultural reasons. However, research done with women in poor communities shows that women begin having children at a young age and have multiple children because they want to. They don't think that being married and having children have to go hand-in-hand. In fact, some poor women prefer to have children and then spend time getting to know their man. They also think that motherhood before marriage makes sense. A relationship with a child will last, but men often disappoint. According to interviews with the women in poor Philadelphia neighborhoods, marriage often is considered a luxury, but having children is thought to be essential.

Another reason many of our program participants don't marry before motherhood is because so many men in poor communities are incarcerated. In some inner-city communities, as many as one-third of black men are in prison. It may not make sense for a young mother to marry a man who is going to be removed from the community for an extended time. When he returns, his employment prospects and ability to support his child will be limited as a result of his felony background.

In poor communities, many men are relegated to the role of baby daddy. A baby daddy is a man who is the father of a particular child. One day after morning meeting, Cassandra, one of our participants, said to me, "You remember Shawna? She used to be at the Bean Project. She's now with the baby daddy of my daughter's son." In a culture in which it was difficult to talk about who is married to whom, perhaps baby daddy is easier.

For a long time, I still wondered why so many of our participants didn't use birth control. After having children at a young age and having to place their kids in foster care while they were working their way through the corrections system, why wouldn't they try to ensure that they didn't have any more kids? Did birth control go against some moral or social code? Did the women not have access? Most women, including poor women of color, use birth control to prevent unintended pregnancy. The key word here is "unintended." While our program participants typically use birth control, they stop if pressured by a boyfriend. Being told "I want to have a baby by you," is a high form of praise. Additionally, according to research by the authors of *Promises I Can Keep*, the way a young woman reacts to a pregnancy is indicative of her value as a person. If motherhood is the most important thing she'll ever do, not wanting the child is viewed as a personal failure. Even if a pregnancy is not intended, abortion and giving up the child for adoption are not options. Keeping the child no matter what is a sign of maturity and high morals.

Middle-class America can't impose its values on poor women about when and how many children they should have. It's better to focus on improving poor women's access to economic opportunity so that they can attain some means to support themselves and their families. If young women in poor communities can believe that finishing school, going to college and pursuing a career are attainable, the incidence of teen pregnancy may drop and this perpetuation of poverty may break.

CHAPTER 9

THE TIES THAT BIND—HOW FAMILIES HELP, HINDER AND PERPETUATE

In my twenties, when I starting experiencing life beyond my family, I realized there is no such thing as the utopian family. It was very liberating. I certainly knew my family wasn't perfect. My parents had divorced and remarried, and lived in different parts of the country. My three siblings and I had to choose with whom we'd spend holidays. There never was a dramatic break between my siblings and me, but over time this physical separation contributed to emotional divides. At the Bean Project, I have seen how rarely family and perfection go together.

I believe there is always some dysfunction in every family. The question is: how much? The word "family" is laden with so many connotations. For some, "family" represents security and happy memories. For others, especially women I've met at the Bean Project, "family" conjures up painful memories of being unwanted and alone. It is often a family member who introduces a program participant to drugs, setting her on the path of addiction and incarceration. Families also can hinder recovery by triggering the feelings that led to the drug use. I'm frequently surprised at how some people can continue to forgive ongoing heinous behavior through years and years of disappointment. No matter how hurtful an addict's or felon's behavior, family members often feel compelled to forgive them because families are the primary social unit and are essential to our survival. It's remarkable how many families continue to embrace and support the women at the Bean Project.

When Velma came to the Bean Project, she frequently talked about her family, especially about her mom and all that her mother had provided. Velma's sister, a FedEx driver, had been to Women's Bean Project a number of times making deliveries, and when Velma was released from prison to the halfway house, her sister insisted Velma come, check us out and apply for the program. Her timing was perfect; it was summer and we had a number of openings.

Velma's family had been in Denver a long time. Her grandparents owned a house in Five Points, an African American neighborhood, where in the thirties the likes of Duke Ellington and Billie Holiday played and stayed, as they weren't allowed in the white hotels downtown. At that time, the main business strip through the middle of Five Points was referred to as the Harlem of the West. The family was well established, but Velma was always a little rebellious, a tomboy with a sharp wit. When Velma was eighteen, her father was killed by a drunk driver. She began using heroin as a means to cope with the loss. Velma gave birth to a baby girl who died of SIDS. The loss of her father and baby triggered a twenty-two-year odyssey of drug use and incarceration. During this time, Velma told me that she didn't care about anything.

In many ways, it was surprising we hired Velma. After so many years in prison, there was little reason to believe she could adjust to the outside. But her gentle spirit, kindness and determination shone through during her interview. She said that this time was different; she was too old to keep going back to prison and was ready for a new life that involved being an active part of her family, building a relationship with her nephew and enjoying family gatherings. We decided to give her a chance, hoping that she really was ready for a new life outside of drug abuse and prison.

Velma's mother stood by her through years of addiction and incarceration. Janet, Velma's mom, was very proud of her daughter and was thrilled to watch her progress as she moved through the Bean Project program and out of the halfway house. A few months into Velma's tenure at the Bean, Janet and I met in the Bean Project's retail store and stood off in the corner, next to a shelf of Toni's Ten Bean Soup, chatting quietly. I liked her soft-spoken demeanor. I remarked with enthusiasm how well Velma was doing and complimented her on being such a great support for her daughter. A pretty, middle-aged woman—you'd never guess she was the mother of a career felon. Quietly, she described how hard it had been to support Velma over the years when she was in and out of prison.

"How did you do it? I'm sure there were times you were disappointed," I said.

"Many times," Janet replied. Then she told me of a conversation she had had with a parole officer during one of the times that Velma was being released from prison. The parole officer complimented Janet on being present for her daughter's release and said that throughout his career he'd observed that when a man is released from prison, there is always someone waiting for him—a wife, mother, grandmother. But when a woman is released, there rarely is anyone waiting. She has burned all of those bridges. Janet said his comment confirmed her resolve to stand by her daughter despite her long history of mistakes. Janet didn't want her daughter to be one of those women with no one to support her, so she committed to standing by Velma countless times over the twenty-two years.

I remarked that Velma seemed committed to her sobriety and staying out of prison. At work she was reliable, paid close attention to detail and sought out feedback from her supervisor about her performance.

Janet shared: "In the past, every time Velma got out of prison, she'd say, I don't want to go back." This time, Velma told her, "I'm not going back." Janet believed the distinction between these two statements was important and the key to her daughter's future outside of prison.

Velma graduated from the Bean Project after nine months. We had a ceremony for her and three other women who were leaving because they had found jobs. After being presented with her graduation certificate, each woman had the opportunity to say a few words to the group of staff and the volunteer job coaches who had worked with the women throughout their tenure in the program. We all had gathered on the production floor, clustered around a large bulletin board we called the Landing Board. As a part of the graduation ceremony, each graduate places a notecard with her name and the name of her new employer on the board. The graduates spoke first, providing words of encouragement to their colleagues about sticking with their plans to change their lives and focusing on what great things would come next. When it was Velma's turn to speak, she began by saying, "I want you all to know that if I can do this...." Suddenly she stopped speaking and her smiling expression shifted, becoming soft and vulnerable. Janet had walked into the room as Velma was presented her graduation certificate. Velma looked at her mom and began to cry. Janet stepped forward and hugged her daughter, then turned to the women and spoke her own words of encouragement.

"We've had a long road, Velma and I." She leaned into her daughter in a show of unity. "And if my Velma can do this, then so can all of you. Do not give up."

Like Velma, some women at the Bean Project appear to come from high-functioning families but end up in situations that no one could dream possible. Rebellion is normal, but some teenage women take it to an extreme. Patricia is a prime example. A white, middle-class, high school honor student, Patricia started sneaking her father's Chivas when she was twelve, beginning a cycle of alcoholism accompanied by bulimia. She entered rehab for the first time when she graduated from high school with honors and surprised her parents by telling them she needed help because she thought she was "retarded." She got sober long enough to matriculate into college, but dropped out in the first semester when she resumed drinking during a bartending job.

Twenty-odd years later, during her intake interview at the Bean Project, Patricia said that her parents had always been there to support her. They were there when she had her first two children. Her parents raised the kids while Patricia relapsed over and over again and went to rehab too many times to count. They worried about her while she lived on the streets and supported her each time she made a new commitment to sobriety. Over and over, Patricia broke their hearts: when she became homeless, when she contracted hepatitis C from using dirty needles and when she was arrested for felony assault on a police officer for spitting in his face while she was high.

Patricia's wake-up call finally came when she was unable to attend her parent's fiftieth wedding anniversary celebration because she was in jail. For all the times her parents had been there for her, she could not pay them back by being available for the special family celebration. Patricia described that moment as her rock bottom, and the shame of her incarceration would haunt her for a long time.

When Patricia was hired by the Bean Project, she was in her early forties. Her oldest children were in high school, nearing graduation, and still living with Patricia's parents. Patricia also had a younger son from a second marriage. He was five years old and lived with his father in another state. For the first time, Patricia was on her own to create her new life.

Patricia was thin and frail, but focused, when she started working with us. She was very self-conscious because she had lost her hair as a result of interferon treatments for hepatitis. She had just completed the treatment, and her dull brown hair was beginning to grow back in a wispy way. She had watery blue eyes, but there was intensity in them when she volunteered to assist with tasks that distinguished her as being capable of higher-level work, including helping in the accounting department.

After a few months at the Bean Project, Patricia caught up on her payments to the halfway house and was allowed to move into an apartment. She got a roommate so that she could continue to save a portion of every paycheck to buy a car, a symbol of the independence she was struggling to achieve. Once she finally had enough money, she began shopping for inexpensive and reliable options. When she found a vehicle that she thought would work, she arranged to have the owner of the prospective car meet her and her father at the Bean. Her dad was coming to help her check out the car and ensure that it was a good deal. I asked Patricia to be sure to let me know when her dad visited. I knew she was very attached to him, and I looked forward to meeting him.

It was a sunny midsummer day when Patricia's dad arrived at 4:45 p.m., just after she finished work. She brought him to my office and he shook my hand vigorously. My first thought was how cute he was—about five feet, eight inches, with gray hair and reddish, cherubic cheeks. He exuded kindness. As he held onto my hand, he stared intently at me with the light blue eyes that Patricia had inherited.

"Thank you so much for all you are doing for my Patricia! She is doing so well and we are so proud of her!" Tears began to form in his eyes. "Two years is the longest she has ever been sober and it's all because of you. This place is incredible."

I, too, became teary-eyed. "We're very happy to have her here." I was touched by the genuine gratitude and desperation of a parent who so wanted his daughter to be healthy. I could only imagine how hard it had been to stand by her through all of the years she had struggled with her addictions.

Patricia told me her dad had always stood by her, but her mom and four siblings had a harder time being supportive through all of her relapses. Patricia was working very hard to redeem herself with them.

I'd estimate that fewer than 25 percent of women at the Bean Project have family members like Velma's mom and Patricia's dad who await their release and stand at the ready to provide support. I can understand why. After years of disappointment from recurring relapse or incarceration, sometimes the best thing family members can do for themselves is to move on and stop trying to save a woman from her own self-destructive behavior. My guess is that the hardest thing a parent can do is give up on a child, but it may be the only way to avoid getting pulled down by their behavior. Helping an addict who continues to use, commits crimes to support her habit and returns to prison, time after time, allows the addict to control the family. Clearly, families must set boundaries. They might provide emotional support, but they shouldn't provide an addict with money or offer to help in any way that facilitates the drug abuse. And they must be prepared to cut ties with the addict if necessary: if she is violent, brings drugs or alcohol near children or deals drugs from home. Families also may have to abandon an addict because her behavior threatens the family's financial stability.

Velma and Patricia were fortunate—and unusual. Though research indicates that released prisoners generally benefit financially and emotionally from returning to their families and, in fact, rely heavily on their families for immediate housing and support upon release, this often is because they have no other options, not because these relationships are the healthiest for them. Women in particular need the support of parents or siblings because they're less likely to have a significant other. He often is either long gone or incarcerated as well.

Lack of family support can increase the risk of recidivism, particularly for women with histories of abuse. Those who were abused or have other negative family relationships are more likely to end up back in prison. Almost half of women in prison or jail report having experienced physical or sexual abuse before their imprisonment, according to the Department of Justice.

I also watch women at the Bean Project work hard to forgive family members who have caused damage, or to develop the courage to build a new life without a family member. Many of the program participants were harmed emotionally and physically by family members and struggle to move past these experiences. They grew up in environments of addiction, violence or sexual abuse committed by the very family members charged with protecting them.

Just as a family sometimes must make the hard decision to abandon a damaging family member, the women at the Bean Project sometimes must decide that the influence of their family members is too damaging and cut family ties to create a new life—to survive.

Megan was one such woman. I met Megan when she was thirty-five years old. "I don't really know why my sister resents me so much," she explained, "but there are probably a lot of reasons." Megan's mother gave birth to Megan while in prison. Megan's sister was fourteen at the time and was given the baby to care for. Upon release, her mother picked up Megan and left the older sister to live with her grandparents. The grandfather then sexually abused Megan's sister.

Megan said she was certain her sister was angry because their mom left her with their grandparents. And, since Megan's sister wasn't around to witness their mother's relapse, she blamed Megan when their mom began using again. Their mother relapsed many times throughout Megan's childhood.

When Megan was eleven, her sister sold her to a man named Shawn for crack. Megan's mom was too caught up in her own heroin addiction to notice. Shawn took Megan, made her his girlfriend and, apparently, treated her well. Megan's sister returned frequently and threatened to take Megan away unless Shawn gave her more drugs. Shawn always obliged.

"Couldn't he see you were only eleven?" I asked in disbelief.

"I know! Though I was pretty well-developed already when I was eleven. My sister told him I was sixteen, and he believed her. But he should have known because of the things I liked to do. When he'd take me to the mall, I wanted to go play video games. I used to ask him to take me to Water World. He said he wanted to marry me when I turned eighteen." She didn't want him to know her real age; she liked the gifts and attention. Megan said she'd been sexually molested before then, but had never had sex until Shawn took her to a motel room on the first night she was with him.

Selling Megan to Shawn was far from the only cruel thing Megan's sister had done. Her sister used crack and introduced Megan to the drug by forcing the pipe into Megan's mouth when she was eleven and then again when she was a teenager. Shawn was a dealer, not a user, so Megan didn't become an addict until years later, without her sister's help. In hindsight, Megan believes Shawn protected her from even worse experiences during that time. She was with him for over three years. When Shawn discovered her real age, he ended the relationship and Megan was forced to begin life on her own.

Megan was in her early twenties when her mom died of cancer. Megan wanted to rely on her sister for support, but her sister found fault with everything Megan did. Megan's sister would say things like "You look like Mom" and point out how Megan was sitting or chewing just like their mother. Her sister wasn't reminiscing. She pointed out these traits to imply that Megan was worthless and to tear down Megan's self-esteem.

"I finally decided my sister wasn't what I needed in my life," Megan said.

My impression was that Megan was at peace with her decision to end her relationship with her sister and to create a positive life that had eluded her for thirty-five years. She was an adult with three children, ranging in age from seven to seventeen, and she recognized that she needed to get her life together and become emotionally healthy so that she could be a good influence on her own kids. Megan didn't believe this was possible with her sister in her life.

As a child, Leigh also experienced trauma from her family, although when I met her, she was twenty-four and still longing for a healthy relationship with each of her parents. One moment Leigh claimed that she had decided to live without her family. The next moment, she talked about visiting her mom as soon as she was released from the halfway house.

Leigh told me she'd decided that it would be best to dissociate from her family to allow herself to heal and create a life on her own. Her mom, she said, had made a lot of mistakes when Leigh was a child. When I asked what kind of mistakes, Leigh began to recount her childhood. In a very cavalier way, she ran down the litany of errors. "Well, let's see. From when I was born until I was four and a half, I was beaten, molested and lived in a car. My father took off when I was four years old. When I was five, my mom dropped me off in my grandmother's yard and took off."

"Was it better being with your grandmother?"

Leigh laughed. "No. I don't know. It was fine. My grandmother was kind of crazy. She used to strap me to a chair to get me to behave."

After Leigh's dad left, her mom was in a series of abusive relationships while continuing to use meth for many years.

After Leigh had been with her grandmother for a year or so, her mother came back to get her. But there was never stability or structure with her mom. "One night we'd eat dinner at 6 p.m., the next at 9. Sometimes she would wake me up at 2 a.m. to say they were grilling steaks and it was time for dinner." Whether or not she wanted to eat, she was forced to get up. "Then I was supposed to go to school the next day. It was crazy."

Leigh stayed with her mom throughout her childhood. Eventually, her mother and father got clean. Leigh resumed communicating with her father when she was in the midst of her own meth addiction. Though he had gotten clean, he was living with an alcoholic girlfriend.

As she told me the story of her childhood, it was hard to imagine she could feel any obligation to maintain a relationship with her parents. Leigh had been sent to the halfway house as a diversion client. She'd been arrested for possession of meth when she turned herself in to authorities, so her sentence was less harsh than it might otherwise have been. I asked about her plans for after her release from the halfway house.

"My first priority is to buy a car."

I'd never heard of a woman wanting a car before she secured an apartment, so I asked why she was in such a hurry.

"So I can go visit my mom. She lives in Grand Junction now."

Grand Junction is on the opposite side of the state. I reminded Leigh that there are buses that make the trip.

"I don't want to spend $200 or $300 on a bus ticket when I can get a car for $1,000."

"How long of a visit do you think you'll make?" I wondered if the car was also a way to make a quicker escape if the visit didn't go well.

"Oh, a short visit. Maybe three days. I can't be around them for long. My mom married the man who raped me at fifteen. Now they have a daughter who is five. Even though she is clean now, I see her raising my sister the same way, making all of the same mistakes."

I appreciated that Leigh was objective enough to see how her mother was repeating the pattern and wondered how Leigh's sister would fare.

Leigh had said that she'd decided it would be best to dissociate from her parents, but she seemed drawn to her family. Although she was becoming aware that her family wasn't good for her, distancing herself was going to be an ongoing internal battle. When she was released from the halfway house she chose to live with her dad, sleeping on his couch. It lasted only a few weeks. Her father's girlfriend had parties every night, keeping Leigh up until 2 a.m. and making it hard for her to wake up for work every morning. Leigh knew she had to find a healthier living situation and moved to a treatment facility for recovering addicts. She continued to postpone her visit to her mom's home.

What was it going to take for Leigh to decide to break the familial ties that bind? Are others able to do it? A 2003 study by Fitness and Parker had 315 men and women complete a questionnaire that asked them to describe the very worst, most unforgivable thing that a family member could do that would ultimately lead to expulsion from the family. The worse thing that a girl could do was have taboo sex, for instance with her father's friend. For boys, it was criminality and drug addiction. The researchers speculated this is because criminality reduces the child's and the family's status and threatens the overall family structure. Families often feel shame, disappointment and anger toward the person sent to prison. A released prisoner's re-entry into the family can be difficult. The family must forgive and trust. The same study identified deception, betrayal and sexual abuse as the most unforgivable offenses between siblings. (I presume selling one's sister for crack counts as betrayal.) Forty percent of respondents said the worst offense a parent could commit was abandonment. Leaving a five-year-old in someone's yard, even the yard of a family member, seems like abandonment. At a minimum, it is a breach of fundamental rules of parenting. The offenses committed by Megan's sister and Leigh's parents certainly meet the criteria identified in the study as unforgivable and legitimate cause to sever ties. Leigh struggled to permanently disengage herself from her parents. She was drawn to them, perhaps hoping the unhealthy dynamic would eventually change. It is hard to watch a woman be continually disappointed by her family and even worse to see her not recognize unhealthy family interactions because they are so familiar.

I've come to understand that some women have no better option than to create a new life without their damaging family. I also wonder how our program participants' children have handled being abandoned by their mothers—both emotionally, during their addictions, and physically when they are incarcerated. How does this notion of abandonment apply when a woman "abandons" her own family through addiction and incarceration? Most women at the Bean Project have left children while they served time in jail and prison. I don't know specifically how the kids respond—I typically see only the mother's perspective, but this forced dissolution of the families must damage the children.

According to a 2001 fact sheet from The Urban Institute, a

nonpartisan socioeconomic and social policy research organization, prisoners released from state or federal prison facilities were parents to 1.5 million children. If you broaden the impact to include all children of parents who are released from jail and on parole, an additional 1.7 million kids, or more than 3.2 million children altogether, are affected by their parents' actions. When mom goes to prison, kids are often placed with other family members, but siblings are not always kept together. Most children lose significant financial support, and the mother-child relationship is disrupted. The damage done by this abandonment is difficult to heal. When a mother is released, her felony conviction creates challenges to her ability to provide financial support. This results is household incomes that often are insufficient to meet even the most basic needs. Kids end up living in poverty, feeling financially and emotionally insecure. They often are surrounded by the negative influences, such as drugs and crime, that led to their mother's imprisonment, setting them up to repeat the cycle of addiction and crime.

Our program participants say one of the greatest punishments of prison is being separated from their children. They wonder what is happening to their kids and if they will be reunited. The impact on the kids is twofold: first comes the impact when mom is incarcerated, then comes the emotional toll of the reunion when she is released.

Only 20 percent of kids actually see their moms being arrested and taken away. Those who do are usually young and in the sole care of the mother. Older kids often are at school when their moms are arrested. They come home to find an empty home, not knowing where their mom is. As a means of mitigating these stressors on children, the 1997 Adoption and Safe Families Act mandated termination of parental rights if a child is in foster care fifteen or more of the prior twenty-two months. This solution was developed when the problem of parental incarceration was growing, largely due to drug sentencing laws. The number of incarcerated mothers more than doubled from 1991 to 2007, and the number of children with at least one parent in prison increased 82 percent during that same time period. Some of the tough-on-crime policies in recent decades are now starting to be seen as overly punitive and costly since long prison terms further fray the parent-child bond. As a society, we must decide at what point we want to intervene: to decrease the number of moms going to prison in the first place; to provide better support for the mother-child bond when a mom returns from prison; or to permanently remove kids when their mothers are sentenced to long prison terms. The Adoptions and Safe Families Act impacted Monica's family when she went to prison. I sat in the kitchen one morning as Monica baked cookies for a tour group that was arriving that morning. Monica described the double life she'd led in her twenties, alternating between being a banker's wife and a cocaine user and partier. Eventually she crumbled into addiction, her marriage ended with no children and she moved to Colorado to be closer to her parents. She then had two daughters with a boyfriend and, a few years later, entered into a long-term relationship with another man who was an undocumented immigrant from Mexico.

"We were so happy and then I started using again." Monica spoke energetically as she told me her story. "Eventually the police caught me and I went to prison for possession."

When Monica was arrested she told the police she didn't have any family besides her daughters and her husband; she was too ashamed to let her father know she was going to prison. She didn't realize that her boyfriend wouldn't be granted custody of the children while she was in prison. He wasn't their biological father and he had no rights because of his immigration status. As a result, her children went into foster care. A few years later, when they were six and eight years old, they were adopted in a closed adoption, ensuring that Monica wouldn't be able to find them when she eventually was released from prison after four years. Additionally, Monica's father died while she was in prison, not knowing where his daughter and granddaughters had disappeared to. As Monica told me the story of her daughters and how much she missed them, she struggled not to cry. She imagined the agony she had caused her father. While working at the Bean, she was also working hard in counseling to learn how to grieve the loss of her daughters and father. I wondered how Monica's daughters had adjusted to losing their family as a result of their mother's mistakes.

I often try to imagine what life is like for the children of the women we serve. I hear so many stories from women who grew up in poverty and addiction, with family members who damaged them, and I wonder how the intergenerational cycle of poverty, addiction and incarceration can be broken. How can the kids of the women we serve today avoid being clients tomorrow? Some children overcome these challenges and achieve successful, well-adjusted lives, but I wonder what enables them to defy the odds, because they are not only defying the odds; they may also be defying the neural pathways formed during infancy.

The part of our brain that controls fight or flight is fully developed at birth. However, other parts of the brain that help us determine if a frightening stimulus is a real threat don't become fully functional until we are four or five years old. The part of our brain that can fully comprehend the level of threat develops even later, at eleven or older. Our caretakers must help us filter stimuli and help us understand what is truly a threat and what is not. They must teach us how and when to calm down and how to self-regulate. When the caretaker is an addict or otherwise unavailable to provide an environment that soothes an infant, the infant does not gain an understanding of what is life threatening and what is not. The neural pathways in the memory are formed at an unconscious level and affect our actions. Women who experience a family environment like Leigh's, surrounded by addiction from birth, need to work on rewiring their brains to learn to respond differently to stimuli and develop a healthy psyche.

This helps explain why the children of addicts are four times more likely to become addicts. They also are more likely to have multiple addictions, like gambling, sex or food addictions. Even aside from a likely genetic link to addiction, the emotional and psychological damage done to young children who are exposed to addiction makes it likely the cycle will be perpetuated through to the next generation, making addiction a true family illness.

We once filmed a video of Brandi, a recent program graduate, and Olivia, her nine-year-old daughter. Olivia had endured a lifetime of neglect and was wise beyond her nine years. Brandi had multiple piercings and a tendency to wear revealing clothing. Olivia was the picture of nine-year-old innocence in sneakers, jeans and a t-shirt. For the interview, they sat side-by-side on a bench in front of a wall painted with the Bean Project logo.

The years prior to this interview had been difficult for Olivia and her three siblings. They had started out living in a beautiful, upper middle-class home, going to a good school and having everything they ever wanted. Brandi and her husband supported the family lifestyle by dealing drugs. Then Olivia's parents were caught, convicted and sentenced to prison. Brandi was released first, after only nine months, and sentenced to a residential drug treatment and halfway house program. When the video was shot two years later, Olivia was living with her mom and learning to trust her again. In the video, they talked about what it was like after they lost their house and before Brandi was sentenced to residential drug treatment.

"We were living in my car," Brandi said, "trying to make it through each day."

"It was scary because we, me and my brothers and sisters, didn't know what was going to happen," Olivia added.

The interviewer asked Olivia what she thought she wanted to be when she grew up. She answered, "A lawyer." Her mom smiled proudly.

Later, as the interview progressed, Brandi said to her daughter, "I want you to know that you can be anything you want to be, even a lawyer. And I will always be there for you."

Mother and daughter looked into each other's eyes and shared a moment of intimacy as if the camera had faded away. Brandi's expression was one of agony for the pain she'd caused her family. Olivia's was just sad. They became teary as they looked at each other. After a moment, Olivia finally nodded to her, prompting Brandi to look back at the camera. Olivia glanced at the camera and then, for a brief second, looked back at her mom, as if she was trying to verify that what her mother had just said was actually true. Like any child, Olivia was looking to her mom for safety and security. She wanted to be reassured that she'd be taken care of and that everything would be okay.

How do we know Olivia will be okay? The truth is that the pattern of incarceration is likely to be repeated. Children of incarcerated parents are more likely to drop out of school, engage in delinquency and be incarcerated themselves. But it doesn't always happen. Even when there are not parental models, children can develop resiliency if they have at least one positive adult relationship in their lives. Despite poverty and stress, this adult sometimes can help create structure and rules, essential environmental factors for children. Psychologists have tried to understand why this is so. What makes one person turn out okay, living as a well-functioning adult, when another person, with an equally horrific background, does not? What is it about some people that make it possible to break the mold and make the decision to have a different life from their family? Resilience is key.

Resilience is the ability to bounce back in spite of setbacks. It is something that can develop over time, but there are specific characteristics that have been shown to make one resilient. Researchers Wolin and Wolin developed a list of attitudes and qualities that resilient people seem to possess that appear to contribute to building productive lives even after severe adversity and stress during childhood. These people tend to have likable personalities that attract people to them. They are also smart and have a general feeling that their lives are going to work out for them, a sort of innate optimism.

But it seems risky to depend on the possibility that people will be resilient. Instead, we should create better overall support systems— for families of addicts and incarcerated adults, for kids who must be placed into foster care when a mom is incarcerated, and for family units when a mom is released into the community. Without changing the unhealthy family dynamic through better wrap-around family services, all we can expect is generation after generation to follow one another into addiction and incarceration.

CHAPTER 10

RELAPSE—
WHY DRUGS ARE SO SEDUCTIVE

I may be among the least likely people to work with recovering addicts, having had no real experience with drugs, much less addiction. Consequently, I was ill-prepared for working with women in recovery, or for identifying relapse, even when it was happening right under my nose.

We require that women be clean and sober for at least six months before we hire them. Most of our program participants are monitored as part of the terms of their release from prison, so the Bean Project typically doesn't do regular drug testing. However, we do conduct periodic, unannounced drug screens if we suspect drug use. Occasionally, a woman relapses while she is in the program. It often becomes apparent because of a change in her behavior, but sometimes other women bring it to our attention. Recovering addicts are really good at knowing the signs that others are using. I have learned to trust this source of information.

I have witnessed several women relapse. At first each relapse came as a complete surprise, but as I learned more about relapse, I have begun to recognize the early signs. Kalila was my first experience with relapse. Today, I know that she was showing an early sign of relapse when she isolated herself. Kalila and Lorraine lived together in the halfway house and had bonded while working at the Bean. Kalila was about the age of one of Lorraine's daughters, and they took the bus from the halfway house to Women's Bean Project every morning. They walked to the bus stop together, sat next to each other and chatted all the way to work. They bonded further when they both were both trained to work at the front desk and manage the store's cash register. But Kalila suddenly started leaving for work before Lorraine, not waiting, as she had always done, for Lorraine to finish breakfast. Lorraine initially didn't worry about Kalila leaving without her. Kalila always seemed to have a good excuse for why she was out the door earlier; she'd had trouble sleeping, she wanted to enjoy the summer morning, she was ready to leave and wanted to get out of the halfway house. This occurred for a few weeks until one morning Kalila wasn't at work when Lorraine arrived at 8:00, even though she'd left before her. Lorraine was concerned but didn't say anything. Kalila still hadn't arrived at 8:45, when it was time for morning meeting. We all went to the second floor for the meeting as usual. After the meeting, Lorraine went to the front desk to fill in for Kalila, who was on the schedule for that day. When Lorraine conducted the first task, turning on the cash register and counting the drawer to ensure that it contained forty-five dollars to start the day, she realized that the money was missing. Lorraine immediately told her supervisor and they pieced together that Kalila likely had entered the building while we were in morning meeting and stolen the cash from the drawer. She knew we left the back door unlocked during morning meeting, and she knew where the register key was located and how much money she'd find there. Kalila didn't return to the halfway house, and several of the program participants, including Lorraine, began seeing her strung out in the park by our building and hanging out on the streets. Lorraine approached her only once in the park and Kalila confirmed our suspicion, admitting she'd stolen the money exactly how and when we thought. The money she'd stolen had given her what she needed for the first hit to feed her relapse.

Another early sign of relapse I have learned to recognize is a longing for the old life, sometimes called romanticizing the drug. Adrienne was smart, and she knew it. I stopped to talk one day while she worked at one of the hip-high, stainless steel tables, placing cornbread labels onto kraft paper bags. It is tedious work but requires attention to detail to ensure the labels are placed on straight.

"I used to make so much money. I'm basically living in poverty compared to how I used to live," she boasted.

I asked if she had all that money because she sold drugs.

"Yes, but I was really into making meth, more than selling it. I enjoyed finding the recipes on the Internet and making them. I was really good at it. Also, I made my money as a welder."

"Did you use too?"

"I was never an addict. I used it to maintain my weight, just a little bit several times a day." She had become heavyset and talked about how "hot" her body had been in the past. She spoke longingly of her old life and of the white professionals she used to sell meth to. She cooed about how much money she'd made, how awesome her life had been.

Something about Adrienne's stories didn't feel right. I couldn't articulate my concerns, but it struck me as odd that she spoke so fondly about her past. I was accustomed to hearing women reflect on their past with regret about the mistakes they'd made, the time they'd lost and the bad people they believed they had been. I know now that she was showing sure signs of impending relapse—it's called romancing the drug. Not surprisingly, that's exactly what happened. As she neared graduation, Adrienne began making plans to go to a local technical college to get a welding certificate. In preparation, she requested funds from the Bean Project to purchase books for her first set of classes. Our case manager believed this was a good investment and gave the money directly to Adrienne. The day she received the money was the last time we saw Adrienne. After she was gone, I heard from the other program participants that Adrienne had started a new relationship with a woman who was bad news. This woman, according to Adrienne's colleagues, was an active drug user and had been affecting Adrienne's attitude up to the time we'd provided her the money. No one had said anything because they didn't want to snitch.

Another way I have learned to tell if someone is preparing to relapse or has already relapsed is that they begin lie. They lie to themselves and to others. After Monique, a fifty-five-year-old woman, graduated from the program and moved in with her mom, she began blaming her mother for being too strict. Monique had started smoking Black Mamba, a recreational drug that is sometimes sold as incense but which contains synthetic substances similar to, but more potent than what is found in marijuana. Monique's excuse: "It's not illegal." At the time it was considered a legal high, but that later changed. "I'm just burning it, not smoking it," she told her mom, though her mother didn't believe it. Monique stopped showing up for work at a job that, according to her employer, was going well and was a perfect fit for Monique's outgoing personality. After a few weeks of the lies, Monique's mom kicked her out of the house, and Monique became an active crack abuser again. Velma, one of Monique's friends at the Bean Project, called me to say how concerned she was. Monique had no-showed for an appointment with her parole officer, which automatically led to a warrant for her arrest. Velma had hoped to provide support to Monique and was expecting her to return the favor when she graduated. When we talked about Monique's behavior in the days before her relapse and disappearance, Velma and I agreed that we wished that we'd understood that Monique's "crazy" lying was a sign of an impending relapse.

While I've known several women who relapsed, I typically didn't know them well. I was concerned for these women, but I wasn't very affected by their relapse. However, one woman forever changed me and my understanding of relapse.

I met Loretta in the fall of 2003. She was part of the first group I would follow from hire through graduation. Loretta stood out because of her size; she was petite and thin. She had just been released from Tooley Hall halfway house after spending nine months in the La Vista Correctional Facility in Pueblo, Colorado, for crack cocaine possession. Loretta must have been blessed with good genes, because most women say they gain weight while in prison. Loretta had remained thin.

Loretta had a great sense of humor and a playful side. Her quick smile was often interrupted by her guffaw of a laugh. A few months into her tenure as a program participant, the topic of "prison stew" came up while I was sitting with the group in the lunchroom. When Loretta mentioned it, there were lots of nods of recognition. When I asked what prison stew was, I saw mischievous smiles pass between the women. Loretta said, "I will make it for you on Friday."

That Friday, the word had spread that they were making prison stew for me in the kitchen. I was banished until the meal was complete. When it was finally lunch time, I was summoned downstairs from my office to the big lunch table where a place was set for me. At my spot on the grey Formica table was a white plastic, shallow bowl containing an otherworldly, bright reddish-yellowy-orange substance. I recognized the color as coming from the super-hot chips that I had seen women purchase from the vending machine. Because they all smoked, their nicotine-deadened taste buds were not as sensitive as mine to the intensely hot Doritos. I looked around the room and all of the women were smiling, daring me to try their concoction. I stalled, asking for a list of contents: ramen noodles, boiling water, spicy hot Doritos and hot sauce. I asked, "Why is this called prison stew?"

Loretta answered, "It is all food you can buy at the commissary in prison— well, except for the hot sauce. This stuff is more flavorful than the meals they serve."

No doubt, I thought.

I never tried the prison stew, and that really wasn't the point. The women wanted to bring me into their world and this was one way to do it. As we sat at lunch that day, the conversation shifted from prison food to more personal topics. It was that day that I learned Loretta had just been reunited with her eight-year-old son and eleven-year-old daughter, who had been living with Loretta's mother while both of their parents were incarcerated. While Loretta spoke proudly of her children, how well they were doing in school and how much she enjoyed being back with them, I wondered if she was having difficulty re-establishing the relationship or her authority as their mother.

Loretta was one of the few women I met who was in a long-term relationship with a man. She and her husband had known each other since they were teenagers, and, as Loretta once shared, he had always been someone she partied and used drugs with. She spoke of him in the way old married couples speak, with an implied intimacy that comes from many years of knowing each other and accepting the good and the bad. I occasionally heard rumors about other women Loretta's husband had fooled around with. At one point, he was purported to be the baby daddy with another woman in the program, but I never asked Loretta about it. Perhaps I was projecting my embarrassment onto her, but I could not imagine it was something she wanted to speak openly about. She seemed committed to the marriage once her husband was released from prison and the halfway house. They would reunite as a family and rebuild their lives, she told me.

Loretta had been clean for nineteen months when we met. Her story of addiction sounded as though she'd spent many years as a functional addict, maintaining a job within Denver's Department of Human Services. Her addiction eventually became too much for her to keep that job. But she was proud of this track record and often referred to the nine years at that job as evidence for her credibility as an employee.

I asked her why this time was different. Why, after all those years of using, was she able to change?

"This time I am doing it for my kids," she said. "I finally realized my kids need their parents to be around, taking care of them. I know my mom took good care of them, but I worry they are angry with me for leaving them," she confessed.

Loretta was happy to be with her kids and out from under the restrictions of the halfway house. She also reveled in being able to dress in her color-coordinated, always-ironed, neat and tidy wardrobe. Because of her size, Loretta could easily find clothes that fit her at secondhand stores. She had a knack for pulling together outfits that looked neither secondhand nor the wrong size.

After she came to the Bean Project, we also helped Loretta get new glasses to replace the prison-issued pair she avoided wearing. It was obvious she needed glasses; she couldn't see a few feet across the room without correction. I asked her why she had not worn her other glasses, so she brought them in one day to show me. They were plastic, oversized, men's aviator-style frames that were so heavy they would not stay up on her nose. At one point, the nosepiece had cracked, and it was held together with tape. I could not criticize her vanity. Those glasses were hideous.

Loretta's elf-like appearance hid a big personality. Though we didn't consistently celebrate birthdays, the group bought me a cake one year. We convened in the kitchen, and when it came time to sing, everyone started with the maudlin "Happy Birthday" song of yore. Loretta interrupted and belted out the upbeat, "Happy Birthday to Ya" version performed by Stevie Wonder.

Loretta always was willing to educate me when I admitted I had no idea. Since she arrived at work every few days with a surprising new hairdo, I felt comfortable asking her how she accomplished the style transformations. It was then that I learned of the elaborate high-styling possibilities that wigs present. My mom had a wig when I was a child. I associate it with the seventies mod style and can picture the white head on which it sat when she wasn't using it. But I don't remember my mom using it to change her appearance. It was basically the same style she usually wore, a low beehive hairdo, and it just made it easier to appear well-coiffed. Loretta, on the other hand, would arrive one day with a snappy, auburn bob and then a few days later with a brown, shoulder-length shag with red streaks. She always talked about growing out her hair, which was thinning, and I was always shocked at the amount of time she would spend at the beauty shop getting hers done.

Loretta quickly rose to a leadership position among the program participants at the Bean Project because she was willing to work hard and take advantage of all of the opportunities offered. She used the few hours of paid time allotted each week to each program participant for education or training to earn her GED. The day she passed her last test—math—we all were so thrilled for her. She was bursting with pride, hardly able to wait until she got home to tell her children. Through contacts that Women's Bean Project provided, she accessed Legal Aid for help with bankruptcy-related issues, bought a car and received Section 8 housing. Section 8 is a federally funded program that provides families with a subsidy that enables them to pay rent on a sliding scale based on household income. The Section 8 voucher allowed Loretta and her family to finally move out of her mother's house and get a home of their own.

Loretta had been successfully participating in Narcotics Anonymous (NA) before she arrived at the Bean Project. When we met, she exuded faith in God and confidence that she finally was on the right path after so many years of addiction and doing whatever it took to support her crack habit. She attended church every Sunday—often alone because her husband didn't go with her—and got involved with church activities during the week. On the day she reached five years of sobriety, we all rejoiced in her accomplishment, passing around and admiring her five-year NA medallion that joined the others in a place of honor on her keychain. I was proud of her and confident that she was on her way to a new life.

While a program participant, Loretta stood out for her ability to earn the ever-coveted paid day off, which women with five consecutive weeks of perfect attendance receive. With her easy manner and ability to relate, she flowed smoothly into an informal leadership role with her fellow participants, becoming a team leader on the food production line and helping train others and monitor quality control. Loretta did such a great job during her tenure as a program participant that we sought grant money to hire her on a six-month trial basis to serve as a mentor to the women. She already was mentoring women. This just formalized it. At the end of the grant period, we hired her permanently as our first-ever program assistant. Her new role gave Loretta the added responsibility of finding resources to help each program participant meet her basic needs—ensuring they had stable housing, transportation, child care and health care. She was very effective at coaching women to reach their potential. She was their inspiration, their confidante and their mother wrapped into a single, five-foot-one-inch package. She did well advocating for the women, but she struggled with the paperwork that was required of the position. Although had earned her GED, Loretta's reading and writing skills were not strong, and her computer skills were virtually nonexistent.

We received frequent updates about her kids, watching them

grow and marveling at their changes with trite comments like "Look how tall you've gotten!" and "You're getting all grown up!" All the while, Loretta's husband moved from job to job, struggling to maintain employment for reasons that were not entirely clear. There always was something wrong with the work, the supervisor, the location with each job. Loretta and I talked many times about how she wished there was a Men's Bean Project for him. Eventually, he was injured and stopped working entirely, leaving the entire burden for supporting the family on Loretta's shoulders. Despite the stress, she maintained her sobriety and continued to hold her family together.

Loretta's son started getting into trouble for truancy, getting suspended and expelled from several schools until he finally received an Individual Education Plan (IEP) for work he was supposed to do at home. Though it seemed sudden, I am quite sure it was not. Loretta said that it was fortunate her husband wasn't working because he could be home with their son. By then her son was eleven years old and had started smoking pot. When I voiced alarm, Loretta responded, "I told him it's okay as long as he is doing it at home." This was the first time I remember questioning Loretta's judgment.

In the summer of 2008, Loretta's son, who was then thirteen, was involved in an incident with a group of young men who almost beat to death the driver of a car who had accidentally hit one of their friends when he exited a bus and ran into the street. There was likely no way the driver could have seen him, but Loretta's son and his friends became enraged and pulled the driver from his car and attempted to teach him a lesson. When the police arrived, Loretta's son's shoes were confiscated because they were so bloody, likely from kicking the victim so many times. This was not the first time she'd had challenges with her son, but it was much more serious. Her son was the only minor involved in the incident, and he faced possible lockup. Loretta started missing a lot of work, first to take him to court, then saying she needed to help find a school where he could begin attending in the fall because that was the judge's requirement for her son to remain at home.

Over the next month or so, Loretta was frequently absent, always calling in the morning of her absence. As the days progressed, the reasons for her absences became more and more implausible. I didn't realize it at the time. All I really noticed was she was missing a lot of work and not fulfilling her responsibilities to the women. They often asked after her and about when she might help them with a housing referral or enrollment in a GED program as she had promised. While she was following the rules by phoning in her absences, I was concerned about the kind of role model she was being with so much time off.

Around that same time, one of the program participants who had begun attending church with Loretta commented that she hadn't seen much of Loretta.

"Do you mean except for church?" I asked. "Don't the two of you go to church together? Wasn't Loretta giving you a ride every Sunday?"

"Nah, Loretta hasn't been going to church lately," the participant said glumly. "I have been going without her. I found someone else to pick me up."

I thought it odd that Loretta wasn't going to church because she had helped them plan a big anniversary celebration only a few months before. She had told me about the elaborate event and the frequent planning meetings. I made a note to ask her about it the next time I saw her.

One September morning, I was walking out of the room after morning meeting. That day I had been sitting at the tables farthest from the door. Per usual, everyone filed out, taking the opportunity to socialize while moving along. With twenty program participants and at least eight staff members leaving the room through a single doorway, I was walking slowly enough that I had the chance to look at Loretta. I was happy to see her for the first time in over a week.

Loretta was standing, bent over a table, propped on her elbows, talking to one of the women. I could not hear what they were discussing, but their hushed tones didn't surprise me. Loretta often spoke privately with the women. I glanced down as I passed and couldn't help but notice that her clothes, typically so well-fitted on her petite frame, were hanging on her. Just then, Loretta stood up and turned toward me.

"Loretta, the situation with your son. Pretty stressful, huh?" I probed.

"Yeah," Loretta replied, a little too quickly. "It's hard. I'm not sure what to do. He was with those older boys…." her voice trailed off.

"Are you okay? You look like you've lost a lot of weight." For the first time in all the years I'd known her, Loretta wouldn't look me in the eye.

"I'm really worried about my son," she repeated.

"Well, you need to take care of yourself too." I reached out and touched her arm, trying to get her to look at me. When finally she looked up I noticed that her normally beautiful, smooth, mocha-colored complexion that I had always admired was blotchy. Her eyes were red and vacant. I could see no Loretta in them. It was clear from her expression that the conversation was over. Reluctantly, I walked out of the room and it hit me: She has relapsed.

I can't say how I knew, but I did. I immediately went to Bob, Loretta's supervisor. Not wanting to face the emotional implications of a staff member's relapse, I addressed the human resource implications. "I think Loretta is using and we need to be prepared for how we will handle the situation."

"Loretta? No, she is just worried about her son," Bob insisted. "She has come too far."

I agreed because I wanted to believe it was true. Not Loretta. Not after being sober for so long. I let it go that day.

But that was the beginning of the end. Over the next month, Loretta started missing even more work, for reasons that were less and less plausible. Several times each week she would call in the morning and say she'd be late because she had one errand or another to run. She called in sick frequently, but would return the next day with little detail about her ailments and dismissed the idea that perhaps she should see her doctor. By the beginning of October, Loretta's attendance was so spotty that Bob was compelled to sit her down late one Friday afternoon to talk, try to help and require that her attendance improve immediately. Still none of us wanted to believe this was related to a relapse—until the following Tuesday morning, when we had no choice.

The phone calls from Loretta started a few minutes before 8 a.m., her appointed time of arrival to work. Between 7:55 and 11 a.m., she called a dozen times, each time asking to speak with Bob. He refused to answer the phone, not wanting to give her the opportunity to make an excuse for not coming in. Sometime mid-morning, he forwarded to me a few of Loretta's voicemail messages. In them, she started with a sigh, "Bob, I still need to take my car into the shop, but I don't want to get into trouble, so I want to talk with you before I take it...."

The messages sounded a little like Loretta, but oddly vacant of emotion. Even though her words expressed concern, her voice did not. In each message she sounded increasingly agitated. It was an odd contradiction. I found myself questioning the logic of calling for several hours to say she needed to drop off her car, rather than just dropping it off and coming to work. Then I reflected on the numerous conversations I'd had recently with staff members who knew Loretta well. It seemed we were all focused on why one excuse or the other didn't make logical sense.

At 1 p.m. Loretta arrived driving her own car, with her husband in the passenger seat, and walked into the building with a boisterous swagger, laughing and talking loudly. Everything about her shouted, "I'm high!" Bob immediately intervened, recruited another staff member and directed Loretta out the back door, telling her they were taking her for a drug test. She stopped them short by saying that it wasn't necessary, she was using again. Bob sent her home and asked her to call in the next morning so that we would have time to develop a plan.

That afternoon, feeling shaky from Loretta's visit, we had a telephone conversation with our outsourced human resource experts. We developed a plan to allow Loretta to continue working at the Bean Project while attending a treatment program. Bob called Loretta and asked her to come in Thursday morning at 8 a.m. to discuss the plan. We anxiously anticipated the next morning.

Thursday arrived and Loretta called a few minutes before the appointed arrival time asking to postpone the meeting to another day. Bob warned that she would no longer be employed at the Bean Project if she did not come in as agreed. She reiterated she was not able to come in, this time saying it was because she had to take her son to an appointment. Knowing that rescheduling the meeting would not change its outcome, Bob told Loretta that she would be fired if she didn't come in as agreed. She never arrived.

I wasn't in the office when Loretta was supposed to come in for her meeting with Bob. When I arrived at the Bean Project, my first stop was Bob's office door to see how his meeting with Loretta had gone. I still was hopeful that everything would work out. I returned to my office, dejected. Loretta had seen what her life could be like without drugs. How could she give that all up? I wondered if I would ever understand the mind of an addict.

Then my mind went to her kids. What was happening with them? If I felt so devastated about their mother's relapse, I could only imagine what they were feeling. My sympathy mostly went out to Loretta's daughter, who had just started her sophomore year at a nearby high school. According to Loretta, she was a good student and active in school. I thought it was probably already too late for her son. He was headed for more trouble and it was getting serious. But Loretta's daughter, Quiana, was a different story.

I tried to imagine what systems were in place to help Quiana and wondered how I could reach out to her and maybe prevent what I didn't want to accept: the inevitability of her repeating Loretta's mistakes. Was it appropriate for me to get involved? Wasn't it crossing some line? After all, Loretta was an employee, or had been an employee. But I was invested in her family. In the past five years I had watched her kids grow up. I had heard Loretta bursting with pride as she told me stories about Quiana, how well she was doing in school and how much she liked high school.

When I was in high school, the counseling center was the safe place, the haven for students with problems. I wondered if that was still the case and whether my experience would translate to the large, inner-city high school Quiana attended. Finally, I decided it didn't matter. I had to try. Quiana deserved a chance and I needed to do it for the Loretta I used to know.

I closed my office door and went online to look up the phone number for East High School. I dialed, figuring that if I could get someone to answer the phone, I could find a counselor. Someone in the administrative office answered right away and transferred me without question to the counseling center. Emboldened, I took a breath, expecting to leave a message. But the phone was answered on the second ring.

I hoped I could leverage the Bean Project's reputation in the community, and started with, "Hi. I am Tamra Ryan, the CEO of Women's Bean Project. I don't know what the protocol is, but I am wondering if I can speak with a counselor about one of your students—the daughter of one of our employees here." I tried to breathe as I realized my hands were shaking.

"What is the student's name?" asked the voice on the other end.

"Quiana Robinson." I told the voice.

"Let me transfer you to her counselor."

"Hi, this is Julio. How can I help you?" The counselor sounded suspicious.

Quickly, I tried to review what I thought were the most pertinent details. That Quiana's mom had been first a program participant and then an employee at Women's Bean Project. As I spoke I began to get choked up. Emotion I was trying to push down was bubbling to the surface.

"Are you talking about Loretta?" he interjected.

I felt relieved. Ok, maybe this wasn't as anonymous as I worried it might be. He actually knew Quiana's mother's name. Who cared that he probably had done a search in his computer to find the information? I felt grounded, as though I had permission to tell him more, including that Loretta recently had relapsed and we had terminated her. I told him I was worried about Quiana and her ability to stay in school with her mom using. I wasn't sure if the family could keep their subsidized housing if Loretta wasn't working.

While I attempted to provide only pertinent details, I struggled to keep my voice steady. Worried that tears would hurt my credibility with this stranger, I paused every few sentences to breathe and collect myself. Yet my voice trembled.

"I'm sorry, I've known Loretta and Quiana a long time. I would hate for Quiana to follow Loretta's path. From everything I know of Quiana, it seems as though she has a chance to have a different life." I also mentioned that if Loretta was no longer employed, they were at risk of losing their housing subsidy, meaning the family could be without a home.

"Well, if they do become homeless, I can connect Quiana with a mentor from Goodwill." He offered, but seemed unconcerned.

It didn't feel like much. "Well, maybe you could check in with Quiana and see how she is doing. Loretta has been using for at least a couple of months. I have to imagine it is affecting her." He agreed to see what he could do. I didn't know if I even had the right to call the school. Perhaps I was burdened with too much knowledge. But

I couldn't imagine not trying something.

In the first few months after she was fired, Loretta stopped by the Bean Project occasionally to see everyone and to brag about what was happening in her life. Each time she came for her fifteen-minute visit, she looked more skeletal and hyped, constantly answering her cell phone, even in the middle of conversations. She also spent a fair amount of time blaming Bob for her firing, saying he had not believed in her or given her a chance, and she had been fired unfairly. We all agreed it was obvious she was dealing drugs again, constantly answering her cell phone to make sure she didn't miss a deal. We guessed she was doing it to support her habit—and likely her family, since she had been the primary breadwinner. Each time, we noted that she still had her car and her nails were manicured, telling us that she had enough money to maintain some aspects of her lifestyle.

The staff was depressed every time she left. We didn't recognize the whirlwind we had just witnessed as the person we once knew, respected and even loved. One day she arrived in the driveway. When a couple of people went out to say hello, Loretta announced with glee that she was going to be a grandmother. Quiana, by then sixteen, was pregnant. Loretta mentioned that her husband was happy because they could collect more welfare once the baby was born. I felt so deflated. If there was one thing I'd hoped to prevent, it was exactly this. Eventually, I asked Loretta to stop visiting. Her drug dealing was a risk to the women in the program, and we were just not up to it.

I can dissect this experience today and see many indications that a relapse was coming. When Loretta's husband lost his job and her son got into trouble, it caused huge additional burdens for her. There were signs when she stopped going to church and NA meetings. She was well on her way when she began the crazy lying.

Loretta's story matters to me because she broke my heart. She was more than just a program graduate. She was a coworker and a friend. I thought I knew her struggles and her triumphs. I was so proud of her and all she had accomplished. I was invested in her success and put her up on a pedestal. If Loretta could overcome so many years of addiction and come out of it together, she was a role model for every woman who came to the Bean Project.

I never understood how tenuous recovery can be and how relapse happens. Some days, I wonder what I did to contribute to the relapse. Other days, I am so angry with her for throwing it all away and for setting her kids up to repeat her mistakes.

I know that I could not have kept Loretta from relapsing. To the extent that we control anything at the Bean Project, we control only eight hours a day, leaving sixteen other hours in which the wheels can come off. But I do wonder what might have happened if I had forced the issue when I first became suspicious of her drug use. What if I had insisted, despite the objections, that we do a drug test immediately? What if we had identified the problem and tried to convince her to go to treatment before it got out of hand? Was there such a time? Was it my responsibility? I still don't know the answer.

What I do know is that I can't take responsibility for someone else's drug use, regardless of who they are. Ultimately an addict's choice to stay clean or use is theirs. Each of us can be prepared to help when the addict is ready for sobriety, but we must also be prepared to walk away when they are not.

CHAPTER 11

THE WOMEN AND THEIR CRIMES—
FIGHTING THE BIAS AGAINST FELONS

Nearly every woman hired by Women's Bean Project has a criminal conviction—or several. It was never our intent to employ so many felons. Our founder, Jossy Eyre, was moved by the needs of homeless women she encountered while volunteering at a daytime shelter for women and kids. She observed the interrelation between chronic unemployment and chronic homelessness and determined that one couldn't be solved without addressing the other. By the time I arrived as CEO, the landscape had shifted. The Welfare to Work act had worked, moving employable women and families off the welfare rolls and into jobs. The women who still had difficulty getting and keeping employment had more complex issues, and a felony background was one of the biggest barriers to finding meaningful employment.

During morning meeting, I sometimes look around the room at program participants and mentally tick off their stories. This one killed her abusive husband. That one used to steal cars. That one was convicted of organized crime. These are typical examples of the crimes represented at the Bean Project, and yet, when I look around the room, I also see seemingly typical women of all shapes, sizes, and skin and hair color. None of these women look like what I used to think a felon should look like, or act like I'd always imagined criminals would act. They aren't dirty or unkempt. They avoid eye contact, but it doesn't seem criminal. It's a symptom of shame or low self-esteem. They are women who care about their appearance, who are embarrassed about their past and who want to have a future with their families. These women have different stories and varied backgrounds, but our society often sees them only as felons. A felon is labeled for life. A felony conviction impacts almost every aspect of a woman's life, from housing to voting, from education to employment.

I wonder how these women can ever create new lives for themselves and their families if society sees them as I did before I began working at Women's Bean Project. How can they overcome these biases?

The Bean Project exists to provide these women with the opportunity to prove that they are not their crimes or addictions. Zenith embezzled nearly $300k from her former employer. Did that mean she shouldn't work at our front desk, operate our cash register and open our mail? Florence had been convicted of killing her abusive husband, stabbing him in the back one evening to save her own life. Did that mean she shouldn't work in our kitchen, using sharp knives? Kesi was a cocaine and gambling addict. Could we trust her judgment in our shipping department? They are mothers and wives and recovering addicts. They were abused and made bad decisions. Many were involved with a man who was active in the drug trade. Sometimes, when arrested, they were just along for the ride. Other times, their boyfriend introduced them to the drugs and they needed to hang around for the next fix. Their crimes are related to their addictions, not because they are bad people.

Before working at the Bean Project, I had plenty of prejudices about felons. I thought felons were bad people who made even worse decisions. In my mind, they existed in another world that affected me only indirectly, and only because of the cost of their criminality on the community. When I was hired to be CEO of Women's Bean Project, I considered myself relatively open minded and felt very comfortable with my attitudes and opinions. But my opinions were rarely challenged. I believed that it was the bad people in the poor neighborhoods, the people of color, who committed the crimes and used the drugs. We could make our communities safer if we locked away these bad people. And look how easy these people are to catch. They stand out there on the street corners! They prostitute themselves. They are a menace!

I never said it aloud, mostly because I had no reason to. My life was so insular that I merely would have been stating an opinion I assumed all my peers shared. Everything I knew about the criminal justice system I learned from television. I now know that America incarcerates more people as a percentage of our population than any country in the world. Although the United States has just five percent of the world's population, we incarcerate almost 25 percent of all of the world's prisoners. Incarceration rates for men had grown during the decade before I started to work at the Bean Project. In some poor inner-city communities, as much as one third of all black men were incarcerated, and, because of drug sentencing laws, the female inmate population was at an all-time high. Between

1977 and 2004, there was a 757 percent increase in the number of incarcerated women. In the nineties alone, the number of women in the criminal justice system doubled.

As I began to try to understand why so many women we were hiring had histories of addiction and felony backgrounds, the facts contradicted my opinion that these women were merely bad people. People of color are not more likely to sell drugs than white people, despite the fact that they are disproportionately represented in the criminal justice system. Without realizing it, I believed the myths perpetuated by the War on Drugs. Not the War on Drugs we hear about today—a war against trafficking from countries like Mexico or Columbia—but the war waged right here in America. That war began in the sixties during President Johnson's administration, when there was a lot of concern about busing, desegregation and affirmative action. The administration proclaimed a war on drugs to try to alleviate the social unrest, even though drug crime was declining at the time. It was a sort of "Look over there!" strategy that served to get the white majority focused on inner-city people of color as the source of all societal woes. Crack cocaine was a boon to the war because it was a cheaper, inner-city drug and believed to be more potent and more addictive than powder cocaine. Research later proved this to be untrue, but in the meantime, it provided a focal point on inner-city drug crimes.

Subsequent presidents from both parties, all the way to President Clinton, upped the ante and eventually created a 100:1 sentencing disparity between convictions for crack and convictions for powder cocaine possession. This supposed difference in potency was blamed for inner-city crime rates. A person convicted of possessing five grams of crack cocaine received a mandatory sentence of five years in prison, but five hundred grams were required for a person convicted of possessing powder cocaine to receive the same five-year sentence. The result, by 1998, was a tremendous difference in the sentencing of black and white people. Organizations like the Colorado Coalition for Criminal Justice Reform (CCJRC) were founded to change these racially biased laws. The Fair Sentencing Act, enacted in 2010, decreased the disparity to 18:1, but the damage was done. While only 13 percent of drug users are black, they account for almost three-fourths of the people sent to prison for drug possession.

Once I learned the history, my experiences at Women's Bean Project began to make sense. Nearly every woman we hired was a felon, and nearly all were recovering addicts. As I got to know the women at the Bean Project, I learned about the female prison population, and I found they aren't the menaces we all might like to believe.

Women who go to prison are much less likely than their male counterparts to have committed a violent crime. Ninety percent of homicides are committed by men. Only about 14 percent of women who are incarcerated are violent offenders. The violent crimes committed by women typically are against a spouse, ex-spouse or boyfriend. It is likely that the woman was physically or sexually abused by the person she assaults. Women rarely commit crimes of violence against the general public.

Though Kristi ended up in prison, it was hard not to laugh when she described a disagreement with her former boyfriend.

"He made me so mad, so I shot at him." Kristi's feather brown hair, smiling brown eyes and innocent voice made her seem almost comedic.

"Kristi! You shot a gun at him? Were you sober?"

"No, I was drunk, but God must have been looking out for him that day. I shot at him six times and not a single bullet hit him."

Not all the crimes committed by women during their addiction were as harmless.

We hired Marli in 2009. I knew she'd been a meth addict but didn't know much else about her until we drove together to a promotional event. As we entered the highway and headed north in my Lexus SUV, Marli said, almost as though musing to herself, "I used to drive a Lexus. One of the sedans. It was fast. That's why I got stopped. Driving too fast. That's when they found guns in my trunk and I was arrested."

Not what I was expecting. "Did you know there were guns in your trunk?" For an instant I imagined unfortunate Marli, just driving too fast, getting stopped and finding out that someone had set her up by using her trunk for their gun stash.

"Uh, yeah." Marli replied. She proceeded to describe her life as a desperate meth addict who turned to gun running to support her habit. Customers approached her with requests for specific guns. She knew where she could get them and for how much and made a hefty profit.

"Did you ever think about what the guns you sold were being used for?" I asked.

"Not at the time." She shifted in her seat, looking out the window. She said she didn't care about anything else at the time, but now that she has a child she wonders about the impact her crimes had on others. Now that she was clean she knew she wanted her child to be safe from people like her former self.

It is unusual to meet a program participant who went to prison for a crime of violence. So why do so many women go to prison?

Nearly all the women I meet committed their crimes while high or intoxicated, or while trying to make money to support their habits and their families. My experience is consistent with the statistics. Most female offenders have a history of drug use and drug-related offenses. In a survey of female inmates, more than half said they engaged in illicit drug use; by comparison, in the general population of women, only four percent use illicit drugs. Carla was extremely deferential, always calling me ma'am and stepping aside when I walked past her, even if there was plenty of room for both of us. "We have to let the halfway house staff go first," she told me once with a shrug when I encouraged her to walk through a doorway ahead of me. Her blue eyes looked watery and tired, as though she had long ago resigned herself to the indignities she'd brought upon herself through her addiction and criminal conviction. Her addiction history was well documented during her intake interview, but I was not clear what had led to her felony conviction.

"I spit on a cop. I was high and living on the streets, and the cop was trying to get me to move. When he grabbed my arm, I spit at him." The edges of her face crumpled as she spoke and she pulled the sides of her sweater across herself. Sober Carla was not a threat to anyone, but she would pay for the aggression she had displayed as Addict Carla for a long time.

Although most women who are incarcerated have used drugs, they rarely play a substantial role in drug trafficking. Most of their drug convictions are for personal use or petty sales to support their drug habit. The Center for Substance Abuse Treatment found that up to 80 percent of offenders in some state prisons have severe, long-standing substance abuse problems. I'd always thought prison was a cure for substance abuse problems. Velma told me that during her initial visits to prison in the late eighties and early nineties, she could easily get heroin, her drug of choice, brought into the prison by visitors and guards. She continued using when released from prison, violating her parole and ensuring that she'd return to prison again and again.

More than half of the women will need substance abuse treatment when released from prison. The Center for Substance Abuse Treatment has collected evidence that effective substance abuse treatment empowers female felons to overcome their addictions, and lead crime-free and productive lives. According to the United States Department of Justice, the typical female offender is a woman of color, between twenty-five and twenty-nine years of age, unmarried, with one to three children. She likely is a victim of sexual abuse, which probably happened during childhood. She often also is a victim of physical abuse; a current abuser of drugs, alcohol or both; and has multiple arrests. Her first arrest probably happened when she was around fifteen years old. She is a high school dropout, lives on welfare, has low skill level and has worked mainly low-wage jobs. These characteristics are disconcerting. How does a woman with all of these barriers gain the ability to change her life without assistance? Without someone being willing to give her another chance, how is change possible?

As the rate of incarceration increased in the wake of drug sentencing laws, so, too, did the number of women rejoining the community and trying to get their lives back. Despite the statistics, the women I meet—felons, former gang members and recovering addicts—aren't threatening and are no menace to society. Often, when I sit and talk with a program participant, I'm struck by how her story and her current persona don't jive.

Kesi was such a woman. She was a stocky woman with closely cropped hair and a broad, bright smile. Though frequently mistaken for a man, she seemed comfortable with herself and her appearance. One morning in our shipping and receiving department, Kesi described her past. She had two children before she recognized that she preferred to be in a lesbian relationship. While in that relationship, she used cocaine and gambled, and was cruel and verbally abusive to her partner.

"Oh, I used to be mean."

"Really? Because mean doesn't seem like you."

"I was using cocaine and gambling. Everything made me angry. I walked around feeling rage all the time."

I remember reading once that we all have an underlying rage, but most of us are able to manage it. "What caused this anger? Did something happen?"

"No, nothing happened. I was just angry because I was defensive. I had no self-esteem because I was an addict."

"So you knew what you were doing was wrong, but you didn't want people—like your wife—to question you?"

"At first I didn't believe it was wrong. I was using cocaine. It was a high-class drug. I was high class and hanging out with high-class people." She explained that high class meant that she could afford the cocaine, she could buy things. "I wasn't a low-class crackhead. I thought, if they can do it, I can." It took about six months of recreational use before Kesi needed cocaine every day. Her wife didn't know anything about the drugs. She thought Kesi just had a gambling problem. Kesi took her paychecks straight to the casino and cashed them. Then she'd call her drug dealer and he'd deliver right to the casino. She would stay all night, using, drinking free alcohol and gambling. She eventually began forging checks and picking up dancers at clubs to cash them for her, paying them with drugs. Kesi smiled as she told me the story, and I looked at her trying to imagine the mean, angry person she described. I wasn't able to locate that Kesi in the warm, friendly and honest face I was looking into.

Kesi reflected, "The people I used to know wouldn't recognize me now. No one ever saw me smile." I asked what they would have said if they had seen her smile. "That nigga don't know how to get no money." We laughed together.

How could I reconcile the difference between the Kesi she described and the one I knew? I frequently have this experience. Women describe their backgrounds, and I have to shake my head to remind myself that the woman speaking is nothing like the person she was in her addiction. More often than not, I find myself saying, "You? No way, you did that?"

I'm fortunate because I get to know the women while I learn about their backgrounds. I can look them in the eye and see their sincerity and their genuine desire to create a new life. But most of society can't do this. What they see, when a woman applies for housing or employment, is the litany of aliases, charges and convictions on her background check. Often their histories eliminate opportunities before the women have a chance to make a case for themselves. This was Stephanie's challenge when she looked for an affordable apartment.

Stephanie was only twenty-two when she was hired at the Bean. She wasn't very likable at first. She had an air about her that implied that she'd been coddled and had gotten her way much of the time, and that she expected nothing less at the Bean Project. She applied to work for us because her father had referred her. He hoped the program would help his out-of-control princess finally gain some of the skills needed for employment so that she could someday support herself and her son.

Stephanie wasn't always pleasant, to either the staff or her co-workers, but she made personal progress, coming to work consistently and punctually, and doing a good job while there. She demonstrated seriousness by setting a goal to get an apartment and then broke down that goal into the tasks that she'd need to accomplish to meet it — saving money, paying restitution and applying for a housing subsidy so that she could afford an apartment on her meager wages.

Stephanie asked for help finding housing resources, and our staff stepped in. Our case manager connected her with housing resources; she applied for and received a voucher for rent subsidy that made rent affordable. All she had to do was find an apartment that accepted the subsidy. The problem wasn't the availability of apartments. She found and applied for one after another, always getting rejected. Her conviction record also wasn't the problem. She had been convicted of felony assault, which is an acceptable crime for most landlords who accept vouchers. But when prospective landlords received her criminal background report, they saw that Stephanie had been charged with assault with intent to kill. If the charge was such an obstacle for Stephanie, it isn't difficult at all to imagine how hard it is to overcome a felony conviction of this type.

Stephanie's conundrum made me realize how a felony background permanently follows the felon. Is it fair to punish someone for criminal charges for which they were never convicted? Employers see on a woman's application that she is a felon and don't give her a chance to come in for an interview. If she is granted an interview and the employer runs a background check, the woman can be eliminated because of her record. I am acquainted with the women and see the work they do to change. All a prospective employer sees is a woman's record.

The most important factor in a woman's long-term success is the ability to get and maintain employment. After serving lengthy sentences, former inmates are unlikely to have the skills needed to succeed in a competitive job market.

Employer attitudes also must change. A survey conducted by UC Berkeley Law School found that 40 percent of employers either probably or definitely would not hire an applicant with a criminal record. Entire sectors of employment, such as hospitals and schools, are unapproachable for felons I suppose the rationale is that this keeps our most vulnerable people safe, but it also confirms the belief that these women are a threat to safety and a public menace. Unemployment is a much greater cause of crime. Up to 80 percent of formerly incarcerated people are unemployed one year after being released from prison. The number one indicator of re-arrest is being unemployed during the year prior to the arrest. As a result, 36 percent of women recidivate within one year. By three years, nearly half will return to prison.

I don't propose that we should feel sorry for the women at the Bean Project. Most did commit crimes. However, once the label of felon is placed on them, a whole host of factors kick in to undermine their ability to turn their lives around. And turning their lives around is what society is demanding of them. If a woman decides she is ready to change and is taking the steps to create a new life, perhaps we should get behind her and enable her to do what she needs to do to find employment, stay sober and stay out of prison. We mustn't stand in her way. We must give her a chance and not assume that the mistakes she made define who she is now.

I now know that the biases and prejudices I had when I arrived at the Bean Project are part of the problem. Once the sentence is completed and the debt to society is paid, is it fair to continue to punish felons by refusing to hire them, refusing to rent to them, never giving them another chance?

CHAPTER 12

THERE WAS A THIEF—
HOW APPEARANCES DECEIVE

There was a thief at the Bean Project. Sure, there are all kinds of women, with all kinds of backgrounds at Women's Bean Project: thieves, drug dealers, even murderers. But they committed those crimes before they arrived. This was different. In the fall of 2010, for the first time since I had arrived at the Bean Project, someone stole from me.

It was a warm October evening and we were preparing for our Fall Jewelry Party, at which we would unveil our newest jewelry line to our supporters. We had revealed a few of the more striking pieces through social media before the party, but none could be purchased until that evening.

Several staff members were staying late for the party, along with a few program participants, providing an opportunity for them to earn a little extra money. Some of the women responsible for making the jewelry were working, and I was excited for them to be recognized for their handiwork on display.

We bustled about the Bean Project's second floor, a wide-open space with lots of windows and hardwood floors, rearranging furniture to accommodate the anticipated one hundred or so guests. Our hip-high, stainless steel production tables, normally used for basket making, were covered with black velvet and topped with earth-toned jewelry necks, each displaying one of our striking new designs. The effect was elegant.

We had hired a caterer to ensure that the event was festive and our guests stayed to buy jewelry. The smells of barbecue wafted through the building. If nothing else, the food promised to be delicious.

Though we had a large number of RSVPs to the event, I felt my usual nervousness. What if we threw a party and no one came? I found myself fiddling with the little signs, called shelf-talkers, that we had placed strategically around the displays, hoping to entice purchases with helpful hints like "Isn't someone's birthday coming up?" and, "You deserve something special."

We all had changed clothes to complement the necklace we were assigned to model and had freshened up our makeup. Marcia, a member of our staff, was one of the last to go into the bathroom to complete the final styling of her short, blonde hair, reinforcing the cute flip she wore at the ends. In the adjacent room, where the jewelry was stored, two program participants were chatting while they waited for the first guests to arrive. I didn't pay much attention to who else was around. When Marcia finished her preparations, she left the bathroom, forgetting her purse. She hastily returned a few minutes later and checked her wallet; the money she had gotten from the ATM that day was missing.

I'd experienced only happy, bubbly Marcia, so the angry Marcia who came out of the ladies' room was a shock. Her pale skin was flushed and her green eyes blazed. "Everybody freeze! Someone took my money out of my wallet!" she declared. We began quick-firing questions, "Where was it? How much money?" I was a little concerned but made a mental note to avoid the same mistake in the future.

A program participant immediately approached a staff member and proclaimed her innocence, saying that she knew that she and the other program participant, Juli, were the most likely suspects. I dismissed that idea since they weren't the only women with access to the bathroom. Meanwhile, Juli teared up and said that she'd had a gift card stolen from her wallet the day before, but hadn't mentioned it because she didn't want to get anyone in trouble.

Juli's proclamation convinced me that this was more than an isolated incident. I wondered if the problem was widespread among the program participants and no one had spoken up. I believed Juli because I respected her. She always appeared put together, with well-coiffed hair and tastefully applied make up. By that time, several months into her tenure at the Bean Project, I had enjoyed several conversations with Juli. We would chat, sometimes sitting in the conference room for a few minutes after morning meeting or at the jewelry production table in the middle of the workday. She shared that she was the black sheep in her family. No one else had ever gotten into trouble. I knew her sister was caring for her children and that Juli was able to see them frequently when she earned passes from the halfway house. The fact that she earned those passes was a good indication that she had progressed in the halfway house program and was deemed ready for home visits. "I've never used drugs," she told me proudly one day. I was surprised, given her felony background for check and credit card fraud. Her only drug while committing crimes was love. She said she'd just followed her husband while he committed the fraud.

The following Friday evening, I had hired a babysitter because my husband was out of town and I was going out with a girlfriend. As I was preparing to leave home, I checked my wallet, thinking I had enough cash to pay the sitter, but not sure I had enough for dinner. I snapped open my red, hard-sided wallet and found it empty except for a little change. I recalled getting cash just a few days before, compulsively following my dad's advice to never walk around with an empty wallet. My heart lurched. Could it be? Someone had stolen from me too? My wallet had been in my purse in my office all day. My office is located in a dead-end corner of the second floor. There was no reason for anyone to be in that area, except to come to my office. Any time a program participant came to my door to talk to me, she always appeared timid and deferential. Whenever I asked someone to come and see me in my office, she arrived as though summoned to see the principal. It seemed unfathomable that someone had not only come into my office, but also into my purse, then wallet, and taken money. But there was no denying that money was missing.

On Monday morning I talked with Marcia and let her know that I'd also had money stolen. I suggested that she keep an eye on her purse, since her workspace was out in the open. I made the same suggestion privately to all the staff members. That morning at morning meeting with all staff and program participants, when we were asked if there were any announcements, I announced that someone had stolen money from my wallet. There was a collective gasp from the group. Stealing from the CEO! Several women looked at each other and then looked down at the table. I expressed my disappointment and sadness and said that I had hoped they were at the Bean Project to change their lives, not stay the same. "Perhaps you do not realize that we have cameras mounted around the Bean Project. Some you see, and some you do not. I assure you that we will find out who has done this and we will press charges." I hoped this would be a particularly scary threat since a new charge would be a ticket back to prison for most of the women. I wanted everyone to know that I was serious, and I wanted the thief to be afraid to steal again.

In hindsight, the threat about the cameras was silly. The cameras in place were wired to a box in the closet in my office. At one time, before I'd arrived at the Bean Project, the cameras were mostly directed at the doors exiting the building. The box no longer recorded anything, and I'd never thought to address the repairs. The outdated technology didn't seem worth the investment. As for the "cameras you don't see," I'd made that up. I thought it sounded tough at the time, but thinking back, I'm embarrassed that I made a threat that I couldn't follow through on.

Regardless, my speech seemed to not make any difference. A few days later, Luanne, our controller, told me that the daily cash receipts from our onsite retail store had been taken from her office. This was particularly worrisome because all receipts go through the controller's office in one way or another. We decided that she should close her office door whenever she walked out, regardless of the reason or length of time. Without a lot of fanfare, we also announced that no one was allowed in her office if Luanne wasn't present. It felt like a small effort toward solving a bigger problem, but we were unsure what else to do.

Then, Marcia told me that she had been stolen from again. I knew immediately that something was wrong when she called me over one afternoon. The sales team, Geoff and Marcia, sat a few feet from each other, a walk-through space running between their two L-shaped desks. Marcia sat cozily behind a five-drawer horizontal file cabinet and a five-drawer vertical cabinet that created a wall in front of her desk. To the left of her desk was the top end of the banister for the stairs to the first floor production and shipping areas. There was only one way to approach her desk and it was readily visible from most of the second floor. She told me through clenched teeth that her purse had been opened and money removed in the late afternoon, the day before. The lack of privacy in her work area made me think that our thief was becoming more brazen. We all agreed we needed to lock up our purses, though I didn't have anything in my office that locked.

It was disconcerting because I didn't feel any control of the situation. I wasn't accustomed to having so little influence over what happened at the Bean. Individually, I discussed ideas for a sting operation with several staff members. We brainstormed ways we could catch the person by leaving my wallet out in the open and installing hidden webcams. It would have been great to catch the thief in the act, but it also would be at least partly my fault for leaving my wallet in such an easily accessible place. I suppose that is what is so insidious about crime. Though I never asked to be a victim, it was hard not to feel somewhat responsible for my own victimization.

I found myself reeling from the incidents, unable to think clearly about what we should do. I'd always thought of the Bean Project as a safe place. Though we have panic buttons that silently call the police, I was proud that we'd never needed them. We seemed to have created a safe environment within our four walls. While we occasionally had issues with women eating each other's food in the refrigerator, there had been no real issues of theft up to that point. As a staff member, I felt respected and protected. But this situation made me feel vulnerable and paranoid. The staff continued to discuss a plan. We spent a lot of time talking about strategies, but our lack of action probably indicated that we were in denial, reluctant to admit that our environment was not as safe as we once believed.

We assumed the thefts had all been committed by one person. We doubted there was a conspiracy involving others because we suspected that gossip would quickly blow their cover. We thought the culprit worked on the second floor, since it would be unusual for one of the program participants who worked primarily on the first floor to come upstairs and do anything other than use the ladies' room or check her locker.

The worst was yet to come. On a bright clear morning just after Christmas, I bustled into the office late for our all-staff meeting. I hastily set my purse on a chair next to my desk, which was only a few feet from the door. Grabbing a notebook and pen, I walked into the conference room just as the staff meeting was beginning. Since all of the staff were in the meeting, no one was supervising either of the production floors. The meeting ended after forty-five minutes, and I returned and placed my purse in its normal spot under my desk. When it was time for a break, I opened my wallet to get money for the pop machine. My wallet was empty—again. Earlier that day, when I stopped at a bakery to buy a cup of coffee, there had been money in it—a lot of money, more than I typically carried.

Besides having been to the ATM, I had placed money that my kids had received for Christmas into my wallet, intending to deposit it into their bank accounts later that afternoon. I fumed because now my kids were affected. Before my feelings had been hurt because someone had so little respect for the staff. Now I just felt angry.

Without thinking, I went to the production floor outside my office and said, "From now on, no one is allowed in my office." It got quiet. No one said anything. I then said, "All staff work areas are off-limits and if we see anyone going into any office without permission and business to take care of, it will be grounds for termination." Staff members late told me that they overheard the women at the jewelry table talking amongst themselves, whispering, "She thinks one of us did it!"

The next morning, at morning meeting I made the same announcement. "I am sorry that the actions of one person have ruined the situation for everyone," I said, shaking and near tears. "This time, whoever did this didn't just steal from me. They stole from my children."

The afternoon of this announcement, Tina, a program participant whom I barely knew, approached me as I was walking back to my office from the bathroom. I was suspicious about why she wanted to speak with me, but agreed and we went into my office.

Tina was a thirty-eight-year-old mother of four sons. She had begun working at the Bean Project while she was living in a halfway house after eleven months in prison for welfare fraud. Though she was clean and sober for six years when she arrived, years of meth addiction had taken a toll. Her teeth had been corroded into blackened stumps by this toxic drug. She needed eyeglasses badly. I once watched her hold a piece of paper a couple of inches from her eyes in order to read it.

"Can we close the door?" Tina asked.

I gestured to the side chair next to my desk and invited her to sit. The door clicked and I turned my own chair so that I could face her.

"I know who stole your money," she said as soon as I sat down.

"You do?" I asked skeptically. For the first time, I noticed Tina's lovely dark eyes, but I found it hard to focus on them due to her damaged teeth.

"It was Juli. I saw her go into your office when you were in the staff meeting."

I looked at Tina, but didn't say anything, so she quickly proceeded. "I noticed it because I wasn't sure why Juli had a reason to come in here, especially since everyone knew you were in a meeting."

"Why are you telling me this?" I found it hard to believe she would voluntarily snitch on another program participant unless she had an issue with that woman. Perhaps Tina and Juli were feuding?

"Because it isn't fair that this happened to you. The Bean Project does so much for us and I don't think it's right that someone would steal." Tina then provided enough details to make her story believable. She had been sitting alone at one of the tables, making bows for our gift baskets, and something out of the corner of her eye that caught her attention. When she looked over, she noticed Juli walking into my office, even though Tina knew I was in the staff meeting. A few moments later, Juli walked out empty-handed and went back to her work station at the jewelry production table.

I was in a bind. I wasn't sure if I could trust Tina, and I couldn't prove that Juli was the thief. I didn't feel I had enough information to take action since only one witness had come forward. I suspected others had either seen Juli steal or knew what she had done, or possibly helped, but no one spoke up. The moral code against snitching is all-powerful. The Department of Justice published a study documenting how the stigma against snitching has become a major obstacle for inner-city police. I was surprised that Tina would ignore such a basic rule of the streets.

In his book *Blink*, Malcolm Gladwell talks about how we form opinions in the first two seconds after seeing a situation or person. These impressions and decisions serve to protect us. We're told to trust our gut. If a situation feels unsafe, we should respect the feeling. In general, this gut-trusting mentality had served me well. It certainly had enabled me to feel safe when I lived in the big-city environments of New York and Chicago, had assisted with many business decisions and generally made me confident about my judgment of people.

In a study published in *Psychological Science,* researchers describe how people make inferences about other's personal traits based on facial appearances. They tested traits of trustworthiness, competence and aggressiveness, among others, and found that we make up our minds after only a 100 millisecond exposure to a face. These impressions often are quite accurate. Were the rules for trusting my impressions of people different at the Bean Project? Was I having difficulty believing Tina because of how she looked? If I had seen her on the street, I likely wouldn't have trusted her, solely on the basis of my first impression. Conversely, I trusted Juli because she looked prettier and more put together.

But I believed Tina. She had nothing to gain by telling me about Juli. In fact, she might have more to lose if she became known as a snitch. I realized I had given Tina short-shrift and had given Juli way too much credit. I had been wowed by Juli's style rather than Tina's willingness to tell what she had seen. I tended to trust people who appeared clean and to distrust those who show signs of addiction. It was a safety mechanism, but perhaps not the most reliable mechanism at the Bean.

I'm embarrassed by this story because at that point, more than seven years into my tenure at Women's Bean Project, I should have been more evolved and understood that first impressions can be deceiving.

If, after all this time, I still could be swayed by appearance, I realized that Tina would face the same discrimination when looking for a job after the Bean Project. I asked Bob, our services director, if he could help Tina get her teeth fixed before she graduated. I wanted to make up for my prejudice. If I couldn't take back my biased reaction, at least I could help prevent Tina from being harmed by similar quick judgment in the future.

As for Juli, I couldn't bring myself to speak to her. Based on Tina's testimony, I felt pretty confident Juli was the thief, but we never confronted her. Juli had admitted to me that she had stolen in her prior life without the influence of drugs, so it seemed plausible that she could do it again. There didn't seem to be any point in confronting her; she had no incentive to tell the truth. A better solution seemed to be to watch her carefully and limit her access to money and to other items that could be stolen. When we did that, the stealing stopped.

We assume that women arrive at the Bean Project ready for change and motivated to create new lives. I believe the women are genuine when they say they want to change, but usually I'm speaking with the clean and sober version of the women. Maybe Juli had just told me what she thought I wanted to hear when she talked about how she was changing her life to be with her kids. A few weeks later, she found another job and left. She had been in the program long enough and had met the requirements for graduation. I didn't attend the ceremony.

I was humbled that I couldn't trust my judgment of a woman based on her appearance or her history. When assumptions that had served me so well produced the wrong results, what am I left with? So many of the biases that drive our actions and opinions are unconscious. I needed to focus on more relevant cues and facts about the women. But what were they?

About a week after I announced in morning meeting said that my kids' Christmas money had been stolen, Velma awarded me the You Rock rock, which is given out at the end of each Friday morning meeting. Originally found in my front yard, the You Rock rock is a dark brown, super-hard dirt clod about the size of a half-loaf of bread, with White-Out lettering on it spelling out "YOU ROCK." The person who wins the rock gets to choose the next recipient and explain why they have chosen that person to receive the award— for being supportive, or being a hard worker or loyal friend. It has become an integral part of the program. While it is touching to hear why someone is given the rock, it is even more heartwarming to see the look on the recipient's face when her name is announced. I've never seen a prouder award winner than the woman who receives the You Rock rock each Friday morning. It is remarkable how something that is worth nothing can be worth so much.

I was honored to receive the rock from Velma. We had developed a friendship since she arrived at the Bean Project after her release from prison. She seemed wizened by her twenty-two years of addiction and prison. She was intense and focused, but calm, and I liked that about her. She always worked hard and was never afraid to pitch in wherever needed.

When she presented me with the rock, Velma also handed me a small white envelope that she encouraged me to open and read aloud. Inside was a note that brought a flashback of high school; a three-hole white sheet of notebook paper, and a ten dollar bill. On the paper in blue ballpoint pen, Velma had written a note. She said that she admired me because I had not fired everyone when the money was stolen from my wallet. "I am grateful to the Bean Project for allowing me the chance to have this opportunity to work and gain many lessons," she wrote. "I realize it is not much, but here is ten dollars for your kids. If someone took something from Daniel [Velma's nephew] I'd be unsure of what to do. I admire you and thank you that you didn't fire us all. You Rock."

I don't know which was more humbling; being reminded of the power of my voice and my position, or Velma giving me money. It hadn't occurred to me that anyone would believe I could have legitimately fired everyone for the thefts.

I tried to give the money back, "I can't take this. Really, please take it back. I appreciate it more than you know, but I can't take it."

Velma stood firm and insisted, "It's not for you. It's for your kids."

CHAPTER 13

ORIENTATION DAY—WHY EMPLOYMENT IS THE SOLUTION

The process for getting hired at the Bean Project begins with an application. Every applicant is required to come to the Bean Project in person and complete her own application. We accept applications all year and hold them until we are hiring. When we are ready to hire, we attempt to contact all the applicants to invite them to come on the appointed day to hear about the requirements for working at Women's Bean Project—attendance, punctuality and a willingness to change their lives, among other things—and what they can expect in return—learning the basic job readiness and life skills needed to get and keep employment.

One sunny morning in mid-June, I arrived at the Bean Project and my stomach lurched. Women stood in line out the door and around the corner, waiting to be admitted. After parking, I walked through the back door and collided with the front of the line of hopefuls waiting to ascend the stairs, check in and receive a name tag with a number.

Women of all shapes, sizes, ages and races were standing, some more patiently than others, for an opportunity to become a program participant at Women's Bean Project. I was greeted mostly with eager smiles. A minority appeared irritated by the wait. I felt the women's eyes follow me as I squeezed by.

The women had heard about the Bean Project in a variety of ways: referrals from halfway houses and program graduates, sent by treatment programs and parole officers. They were felons, recovering addicts, victims of domestic violence. They were all there for one thing, a second chance.

That year Stella, a senior program participant, made the calls. Stella was a beautiful, middle-aged woman with a sturdy build and a sultry voice from years of smoking. She exuded a joie de vivre, despite living in a local halfway house for nearly a year. As she invited applicants to the orientation, Stella coached each one, "Please be here on time because we're gonna close and lock the doors at 8:30. And make sure to turn off your cell phone. Also, there will be a drug test." We grimaced when we overheard Stella warning the applicants about the drug test. We had hoped she wouldn't tell them about the drug test because we wanted to know if they were actively using, but Stella said she couldn't help herself. She wanted to make sure that every woman had a chance. After Stella finished calling the nearly 300 applicants, she had 135 women confirmed to attend the orientation. With every confirmation, Stella provided a mini-pep talk, telling each woman how excited she was for her. Since she made the calls from a desk outside of my office, I enjoyed hearing each call and the enthusiasm in Stella's voice.

I was always impressed by how happy Stella was for others' progress. Because of her long history of addiction and incarceration,

Stella had received a long sentence to the halfway house. It was likely she'd still be living in the halfway house when she graduated from the Bean Project, which would make it tough to find a job in the community. Yet, whenever one of her peers was paroled and moved into her own apartment, Stella was always the loudest cheerleader. She didn't let her own lack of progress get in the way of celebrating others' accomplishments.

In preparation for orientation day, the second floor of the Bean Project was cleared, and every chair, bench and stool in the building was set up. When the women checked in, they received a name tag and number and were asked to sit. All eyes were on me when I opened the program by welcoming the group and congratulating them for taking the first step toward creating a new life. As I spoke, I looked around the room at the hope and fear on the women's faces. Like a Baptist preacher, I witnessed nods when I spoke about the Bean Project being a place to create change. "Perhaps you have reached a point in your life where things aren't working for you and you have no other choice but to create something new for yourself." Nodding. "This is a place I hope you have come to because you are ready to change." More nods.

When I completed my welcome speech, our services director, Bob, reviewed the agenda for the day and broke the sad news. Half of the group would be invited back for an interview and tryout, and less than half of that group would be hired. Ultimately, only twenty women would be offered jobs. Faces fell. The group seemed to deflate. He informed them they'd each have the opportunity to make their case. Each woman would be asked to introduce herself and tell us why she'd like to be hired.

The number of women we hire at any point is determined by

our sales projections and the inventory needed to meet those sales. It's overwhelming to see a roomful of women who want a chance to change their lives and feel that we have failed them because our sales can't justify hiring more.

Maybe knowing that everyone would not be hired helped the woman speak more honestly. One by one, each woman stood, said her name and explained why she wanted to work at the Bean Project. I had to admire their courage as they spoke to a roomful of strangers.

One white woman, with gang tattoos and a severely short haircut said, "No one believes in me any more so I'm starting not to believe in myself."

A soft-spoken Hispanic woman struggled to lift her voice loud enough to be heard, "My daughter idolizes me, but I know I'm not worth that."

A black woman who was boisterous when she arrived became somber as she shared, "I'm really ready for change. I'm not kidding myself any longer."

Over one hundred women stood up and said why they had come. Each rose and publicly proclaimed her intent to change her life. I saw and heard each woman's hope and fear, but my heart ached. Knowing that we could afford to hire only one in five women and seeing so many more women who deserved a chance renewed my commitment to do more.

Our staff members, volunteers and senior program participants took notes while the orientation attendees took turns telling us why they had come. We wrote down our observations, what they said, how they were acting. Did they seem sincere? Were they respectful when others were talking? Afterward, Bob compiled everyone's notes and made decisions about whom to invite back the next day for a one-on-one interview and a chance to work on the production line for thirty minutes.

Requiring that the women return the following day at a specific time creates an additional test of their sincerity. Will she arrive on time? Will she dress appropriately, based on the instructions prohibiting sleeveless shirts or open-toed shoes on the food production floor? Can she take direction while working on the production line?

During the interview, we probe about her background and ask questions about barriers she might have to employment, including child care, housing and transportation. She still may be hired if she is having problems with these basic needs, but it's helpful for us to know what assistance she will require to succeed.

Based on how the work on the production floor and the interview go, a subset of the women are invited to return one last time for a drug test. Once again the women are asked to arrive at a specific time. Our testing company provides a nurse so we can test everyone at once at the Bean Project. When we receive the results and confirm there is no current drug use, we are ready to make offers of employment.

Stella helped call the women who were offered jobs. It was an emotional day for her. She told me that the women screamed and cried when they learned they'd been hired. Stella cried right along with them. Later when I asked Stella why she'd cried, she said, "When I called to tell them they were hired, they acted like they won the lottery."

"It's funny you say they acted like they won the lottery," I said, thinking this was an exaggeration.

"Miss Tamra, they did win the lottery. Everyone knows this is the place you go to change. It works and everybody knows it."

What about the women who weren't hired? Does this experience just fulfill their expectation that nothing is going to change, that they can't get ahead, that even Women's Bean Project, the place to go when you have nowhere else, won't take them in? I fear this is what they think, and I'm saddened we have this effect. I want to tell the women who aren't hired to be patient and apply again. I want to tell them that we hope to hire more women in the future.

Why can't we hire more women? As with any business, employment opportunities at Women's Bean Project are driven by sales. It may sound strange coming from a nonprofit organization, but we are a sales-driven organization. Revenue from sales creates jobs and provides the work that enables us to teach women the job readiness skills needed to maintain employment. When sales grow, we can hire more women and our impact grows.

As a transitional employment program, we hire women who need a stepping stone to move into the workforce. Transitional employment provides temporary, subsidized jobs in a supportive environment to those who lack work experience, education and training. There are several features to transitional employment. It is paid work, but it usually does not pay well. Women at the Bean Project earn eight dollars per hour and receive no traditional employee benefits. What they receive instead is flexibility. As part of our case management, we allow each woman up to five paid hours off each pay period to attend to her basic needs, such as appointments for housing, health care and education. We subsidize her public transportation pass, connect her with dental resources, and help her learn interpersonal skills.

Another key aspect of transitional employment is that it is not make-work. There is a market for the products and they are made to be sold in stores, to be purchased as gifts and to end up on people's dinner tables. The work program participants do is essential to our operations. They assemble the products, stock and staff the retail store, and pack and ship all boxes leaving our facility. They are paid for their work done while they receive real-world training.

A typical woman hired by the Bean Project has never held a job longer than a year. In about nine months she learns basic skills, acquires good workplace behaviors and learns how to apply for unsubsidized jobs. She also learns how to speak more effectively about her background to prospective employers.

Stella was right, our program works. Sixty to seventy percent of our women graduate from the program and find unsubsidized jobs in the community. A year later, 85 percent of these formerly chronically unemployed women are still employed. This means that more women are working, supporting their families, and contributing to society than would have been without our help. But if a temporary job that pays eight dollars per hour can feel like winning the lottery, there must be something wrong. We must have a greater sense of urgency to create more opportunities for women.

We currently hire about seventy women a year and turn away four out of five qualified applicants. That means we aren't able to hire 280 women every year because we don't have the capacity to employ them. And that is only in Denver. There are cities all over the country populated by women struggling with the same challenges. Imagine how many women—and families—could be affected if there were more Women's Bean Projects around the country, if our products could be found in every grocery store in every community. Then we might make a dent in the demand. My greatest wish is that Women's Bean Project will someday put itself out of business. I wish we could provide services so effective and long lasting that the impact would be felt by future generations as well as today. My greatest fear is that in twenty years we will be serving the daughters of the women we serve today. I believe that when we change a woman's life, we change her family's life. By teaching each woman the skills to get and keep employment, we help her become a role model for her children. When a woman learns skills at the Bean Project, her children grow up seeing their mother go to work every day, set goals, manage her money and communicate better with the people around her.

Janine grew up with no role models for employment. She grew up surrounded by her parents' crack addiction. By the time she was twelve, she began selling crack to her parents because she thought it would give her the opportunity to spend more time with them. At sixteen, she began using crack for the same reason. For years, through the births of four children, Janine continued to sell crack and eventually got involved with big time drug dealers. Janine thought she had it made until she was arrested and convicted on federal drug charges and sentenced to fifty-four months in federal prison.

Janine served her sentence, was reunited with her four kids and began working at Women's Bean Project. She successfully completed the program and today is enrolled in college and works for a food distributor, making over seventeen dollars per hour. All four kids, ranging in age from eight to eighteen, live with her, and she is focused on keeping them in school and helping them avoid making the same mistakes she made. She is a role model for employment and education. She has created a new life for her kids.

The children of the women we employ are the future of our community. By helping their mothers change their lives, we affect their children as well and help them become contributors. It is unacceptable to allow generation after generation to become mired in addiction, poverty and incarceration. For our part, Women's Bean Project must grow our sales and significantly increase the number of women we can employ. We must provide services so effective that we stop chronic unemployment in its tracks, reaching into the next generation and preventing the daughters from ever needing our help. I envision a day when women can break out of poverty through employment and the social services system will enhance rather than impede this process.

What our founder, Jossy Eyre, started in 1989, with limited resources and a vision for creating a safe and accepting work environment for women, has expanded into a robust social enterprise and a proven business model for communities across the country. Women's Bean Project has built a legacy of making delicious food products and providing effective services while creating a loyal following of supporters across the country. It is my responsibility to envision and shape the future for the Bean Project and affect the cycle of poverty.

So our work is not done. But the seeds of hope planted in one woman expand to families and communities and touch individuals worldwide. By helping women help themselves, we provide opportunities for our participants to discover their talents and develop skills to join the workforce and build better lives. I believe it is a basic human right to live a stable, healthy life. We are nurturing economic sustainability by enabling women to gain self-worth and self-sufficiency. Acquiring the tools to sustain themselves and their families provides women with a second chance. After all, that's all they are hoping for.

CHAPTER 14

BEAUTIFUL BOY—
WHEN MY LIFE AND WORK COLLIDED

"Now, you understand that after today, this is permanent? He is with your family forever."

It was a hot morning at the end of August, and we sat in the courtroom with family and friends. With the exception of traffic court, I had never been in a courtroom before. It was just as formal as I expected, with a large, officious bench behind which sat the middle-aged female judge, two witness tables and pew-like seats where our friends and family were seated. It had barely been six months since our son had come into our lives.

"Yes, your Honor," my husband and I said in unison.

This was no less than the fourth time she had asked us the question. I suppose the judge had reason to ask. Our son was not yet three and already had been shuffled around to a half-dozen living situations. The judge wanted to be sure we were his forever family. My husband and I sat at the witness table on one side of the courtroom with the permanency case worker, who was responsible for finding a family for Cade, and our four-year-old daughter, who was drawing pictures with a borrowed pencil on a scrap of paper she had found on the floor. Being two years old, Cade could not be bothered with the grown-up talk. He crawled around the floor under our chairs.

We were joined that day by nearly twenty friends and family members who wanted to help us celebrate the new addition to our family. The judge was surprised when so many people filled her courtroom. I commented that we'd been told that we could invite as many people as we liked and so we had. She seemed impressed, and I assumed she didn't often see such an enthusiastic brigade. A judge in a family court does not have the opportunity to do a lot of happy work. Her judgments often are the sad outcomes of poor choices made by people who should be responsible for the well-being of children. This was not the first time Cade's case had come before this particular judge. She had made the judgment that terminated his birth parents' rights, once for his birth mother, who signed away her rights before she went to prison, and a second time for his birth father, who lost his rights by default for failure to meet court-ordered drug testing and parental visitation requirements. In this context, it was not hard to understand why the judge wanted to be certain that we understood that we were signing on to be Cade's family forever.

What this judge didn't know was how unlikely it was that we would be in that courtroom at all. Just nine months earlier, in the fall of 2009, we had been content as a family of three. Our daughter was almost four years old, and my husband and I had determined she would be our only child. With our daughter out of infancy and soon, I hoped, able to entertain herself, I felt our lives were once again under control and predictable. When asked if we planned to have a second child, we would reply, "No, she is one of one."

It had been a stressful six months since our son arrived. For one thing, it happened very fast. It was only seven weeks from the day we found out our son needed a home to when he joined our family. We had developed a new appreciation for the nine-month human gestation period.

Nine months earlier, we had been hiring a supervisor for our nascent jewelry business at Women's Bean Project. We identified a candidate through the county's On the Job Training (OJT) program, which subsidizes the first six months of the employee's wages. Some clients enter the workforce development system because they are trying to transition from welfare to work. If things work well during the OJT period, the employer is obligated to hire the trainee as a permanent employee. One of our favorite case managers identified a woman named Marie and thought she would be perfect for us.

I met Marie on a warm, sunny day in September, the kind of Colorado fall day you wish could last forever. I was the second person to interview Marie, and I could see she was nervous. She kept pulling on the front of her shirt and smoothing it over the top of her black pants. I smiled to try and put her at ease as we sat at the glass conference table in my office. Through the glass I could see her legs bouncing as her foot moved spasmodically. My objective was to get a feel for her stability, seriousness and ability to connect with the women.

As we discussed her most recent work experiences, I noted that she appeared to be in her mid-thirties. "My goal is to break the cycle," she said softly. "I don't want to be on assistance any more. I want to be different from the rest of my family."

I was impressed by her insight, and by her desire to make sure that her twelve-year-old-son grew up differently than she had. I later learned she grew up poor and was bounced back and forth between her divorced parents. Then Marie said something said that made me pay closer attention. "I recently gave my grandson up for adoption." Marie had a daughter who was an addict, and Marie had gained custody of her daughter's child. All I could think to say was, "Wow, that must have been difficult."

"Actually, it was the least selfish thing I've ever done," she said with a sincerity that was impossible to question.

A hundred questions crossed my mind about the circumstances surrounding her grandson, but I had already learned enough. This was a woman with integrity, insight and humility. We finished our meeting by agreeing on a start date.

Once she started, Marie and I quickly settled into a routine. We met for a few minutes every morning to discuss the jewelry business, the program participants, their work and other issues related to the upcoming business launch. We also spent time getting to know one another. In one of our random get-acquainted conversations, Marie mentioned that her Spanish appearance came from her father and that her mother was white. "Her maiden name is even Heberlein," Marie said.

I stopped short. "Wait! That's my maiden name! I've always been told that if I meet someone whose last name is Heberlein, we must be related. How funny would that be if we were related?" My great, great-grandfather had come to America from Prussia in the 1880s and eventually settled in the northeastern part of Colorado. Since we were both in Colorado, it did not seem totally unlikely that we were somehow part of the same family.

We agreed that we would each ask our parents—her mother, my father—if they knew each other. Neither of our parents knew the other, so I let it go, filing away the fun fact that we shared the same family name.

As Marie and I became better acquainted, she began to share the circumstances that led to her giving her grandson up for adoption. Marie had dropped out of high school at seventeen when she gave birth to her daughter. Her daughter followed in Marie's footsteps, dropping out of high school in the eleventh grade. Although Marie was disappointed that her daughter quit school, it was not surprising. A parent's low education level is one of the risk factors for dropping out of school. Marie was happy when her daughter and her high school sweetheart reunited and moved in together when their baby was born three years later. Unfortunately, the young, uneducated parents struggled to find jobs to support themselves. Faced with the pressure of supporting a child, they sold methamphetamine to make ends meet. Soon, they both began using the drug. The couple split up when their baby was just a few months old. The drugs began taking their toll. Marie's daughter would leave the baby with various caretakers while she used. Marie's mom cared for her great-grandson for a while, but she became ill, so he landed in Marie's custody. At the time, Marie already was struggling to get off of welfare and support herself and her son. She wanted her grandson to have a stable life with two parents and decided that the best solution was to give her grandson a fresh start with a new family who could care for him forever. Working with the county, she placed her grandson into foster care with a family she knew. All of this happened just a few months before she started working at the Bean Project.

About three months after she started working for us, Marie came into work visibly upset. She had received a call from her grandson's foster family letting her know that they had notified the department of human services that they needed to place her grandson elsewhere. Sitting in my office, Marie began to cry. I cried along with her.

"He's not a puppy! How can they just decide not to keep him?" I said. I had never even seen this child, but my heart went out to him. Who was this foster family?

"He is so sweet and such a beautiful little boy!" Marie said, overcome with despair. "I just wanted him to find a family with two parents, a family that would take him to museums and the zoo. I want him to go to college."

I'm not sure why the story affected me so much. I was too distracted to work, so I called my husband, Bill. As I told Bill the story, I was surprised to begin crying again. I felt so sorry for this poor child.

Finally Bill said, "You don't need to be crying in your office. Why don't we meet for lunch?"

As we sat at a deli eating our sandwiches, I told Bill more of what Marie had said about the situation. Since I was unfamiliar with how the foster care system worked, my imagination ran wild about how the social workers would go about finding a family, how long it would take, and what would happen in the meantime. Once again, I got teary. I felt helpless and struggled to continue when Bill asked, "What does he look like?" I told him I didn't know, but the picture in my head was of a mini-Marie, without the piercings and the tattoos. I didn't even know his name.

My husband looked across the table at me and said, "Do you think you would want to do it?"

Unsure about what he was referring to, I said, "Do what?"

"Adopt him," he said, as though it were obvious.

I was floored by this question since my husband never had an interest in adoption. When we were getting married and talking about having a family, we decided that we would not pursue adoption even if we were unable to have children. But now we had a child. Perhaps it was the experience of being parents that made us so concerned with the plight of this little boy.

"Well, I don't know," I replied. "I don't know if we could adopt. Maybe. I'm not sure what it would entail." My head was spinning, partly I was confused by Bill's suggestion and partly because it presented a glimmer of hope.

"When you get back to the office, why don't you call the social worker and see?" Bill suggested. "There's no harm in getting more information."

When I walked back into the Bean Project, I passed Marie and asked her quietly if she'd meet me in my office. As she sat down, I began, "I don't want you to think we are being creepy, but what would you think if we tried to adopt your grandson?" It sounded strange even as I said it. Why would we think of adopting a child we'd never even seen? "I think it would be awesome." Marie began to tear up again. I didn't want to cry again, so I cleared my throat and asked if she would give me the social worker's contact information. A few minutes later she returned to my office with a yellow sticky note with the name and phone number of the social worker, Heidi. She also brought her cell phone to show me a picture of her grandson. I saw a beautiful, blond-haired, blue-eyed boy with a somewhat stunned look on his face staring up into the camera. I finally asked his name.

"Cade," Marie replied, surprised she had never mentioned it.

I closed my office door and called Heidi. I explained who I was, how I knew Marie, and that we had heard about Cade and wanted to look into becoming his parents.

Her response was dismissive. "The first thing we need to do is look into whether there are any family members who would be appropriate. Then, if not, we have a lot of families who have already been through foster parent training. He will be very easy to place."

"Would it make any difference to tell you that I think we might be related?"

"Can you prove it?" Heidi asked skeptically.

"Well, no, but I think it may be the case." Feeling just as lame as that sounded, my voice trailed off.

"I will keep your name on file, but we are looking at several relatives for possible placement." The message: Don't call us, we'll call you. Then, almost as an afterthought, Heidi said, "If you really are serious about this, you would have to go through the foster parent class. It lasts for eight weeks and the next one starts January 6." She was quick to point out that completing the class didn't mean we would be selected.

I jotted down the details about the class, which started in three weeks, and hung up. That evening, Bill and I agreed that it would do no harm to sign up for the class. The worst thing that could happen was that it would be unnecessary and we wouldn't attend. I registered the following day.

Over the next several days, Bill peppered me with questions about how the process worked. When would we hear if we were being considered? When would we hear if we weren't? Realizing that I would get no rest from my curious husband, I called Heidi.

"We are looking for a permanent placement for Cade," she said. "We don't want him to have to move again."

"Once you find the placement," I asked, trying to maintain a conversational tone, "how does the process work?" She explained that the law requires that all children be placed into foster care for six months before the adoption can be legally finalized. Once again, she told me that several family members were showing interest, as well as several other prequalified families.

Next thing I knew, it was Christmas and our little family of three was enjoying a festive holiday. Nearly every night, as we were preparing for bed, Bill would say, "I wonder if Cade is having a nice Christmas."

The Monday after Christmas, the phone in my office rang. I was looking forward to a productive day, anticipating that most people wouldn't be working. But Heidi, the social worker, was. "I am calling to see if you understand that our county requires an open adoption and want to make sure you would be okay with that," she asked without explanation.

"Well, I don't know. If it means that a meth addict could show up on our doorstep, then no, we wouldn't be okay with that." I was confused about the reason for Heidi's call, and I immediately thought to protect my family. Even though I had met many women at the Bean Project who were recovering addicts, I still held tightly to my biases about addiction. It was one thing for me to choose to work at Women's Bean Project, but another to involve my family. "No, nothing like that," she explained. "It means that if the birth parents ever wanted to be in contact with Cade, they could, but through our department. You would be able to determine the level of contact you are willing to have."

When I had heard the term "open adoption" in the past, I pictured a family sitting in a park—the adoptive parents, a desperate-looking birth mom and a confused child sitting on a swing, feeling torn loyalties. If an open adoption meant that we had to have a relationship with the birth parents regardless of their condition, I knew we wouldn't be willing to sign up.

Up to this time, my only reference points for adoption were from my own experience as an adoptee. Earlier, when I said I had never before been in a courtroom, it wasn't entirely true. When I was two years old, I was taken to a courtroom and adopted by my father. My birth parents were married and my birth father had left my mother before either of them knew she was pregnant. My mom eventually met the man who became my adoptive father. My mother sat me down one evening when I was eight or nine years old. As we snuggled side by side on the edge of my bed, she explained that my dad had adopted me. He chose me, she emphasized. I hadn't seen this coming and at the time I remember feeling different, rather than chosen. I had three siblings. I realized at that moment that they were all half-siblings.

It wasn't until I was an adult that I learned that my original birth certificate was sealed. I never would have known my birth father's name or my original surname if my mother hadn't told me. I always had assumed that no information was ever made available to either the birth family or the child.

When my mother told me about my birth father, she also told me that I could meet him one day if I wanted. I just needed to let her know and she would make the arrangements. As far as I was concerned, I had a father and I lived with him. I didn't feel a void where a father should be. Later in college, I began to want to know my birth father and decided to meet him, not to fill a fatherly void, but because I thought it might help me know myself better.

All of this was in the back of my head as I replied to Heidi, "I understand what it is like to want to meet a birth family." I briefly shared my story with Heidi. She said there were four different people who said they wanted Cade, but everyone wanted what was best for him. I assured her that that was our motivation as well.

My husband and I rang in the New Year and started the first week of January knowing that we were set to start the foster-parenting class on January 6. We had not received any indication that we shouldn't bother.

Mid-morning on the sixth, I was in my office getting organized, knowing that I would need to leave a little early to pick up our daughter and arrive home in time to make it to the foster-parenting class. A snowstorm was forecast for that evening. Everyone was cautious about their plans for the end of the day. As I focused on replying to emails, my phone rang.

"Tamra, this is Heidi. We've been speaking with Cade's family members and none are interested in taking him. So, you and Bill are it. We're in a time crunch, though. He needs to be in your home by the end of the month."

No words came immediately to mind. I felt exhilarated—we won! I thought about all of the steps to the adoption process that Heidi had told us about, knowing that we hadn't fulfilled any. We hadn't yet started the classes, and yet we were going to be Cade's forever family. Heidi went on to explain that they might still have to consider some waiting families for placement unless we could demonstrate our seriousness by immediately completing the necessary paperwork to get the process started. She was willing to provide some basic information about Cade, including birth and other medical records to demonstrate he had no major health concerns or behavioral issues. Since we were going to class that evening in the same building where her office was located, I agreed to meet her before class and pick up the paperwork she needed us to complete.

I was anxious to call Bill. When I reached him, we spoke excitedly in hushed tones as we reviewed our plan for that evening. As I looked out my office window, the snow began to fall.

By that evening, we were in the midst of a blizzard that only got worse as we drove west to the foster-parenting class and our meeting with Heidi. We received the inch-thick package of paperwork and walked into the classroom. I had difficulty concentrating. Were we really going to become a family of four?

The instructors jumped right in, describing what we could expect over the next eight weeks. I looked around the room at the variety of people, all interested in providing foster care to children. There were same-sex couples, older couples who I imagined had grown children, younger couples, mixed-race couples, and even single people. Sixty people had come to the class, all lined up in rows at training tables, sitting in uncomfortable plastic chairs. I was amazed how many people were interested in being foster parents. That evening was the first of ten courses offered throughout the year. Not everyone in the class planned to adopt, but for those who did, the instructors worked hard to manage their expectations, saying that everyone needed to go into the process prepared to get their hearts broken. They told numerous stories, including some personal experiences, of children who had lived with foster families for extended periods, only to be removed and placed back with the birth mother. They emphasized again and again that the county's priority was the child's best interest. I felt like we were in a room full of people who had bought lottery tickets and our ticket was the one that hit the jackpot. No waiting list, no late night calls for emergency placement. No returns to the birth mother after we had fallen in love. I had no doubt we would be a good placement for Cade, but I felt a little guilty about skipping to the front of the line.

We completed all of the paperwork as quickly as Heidi requested. Over the next several days, while we ran around, getting money orders to pay for our background checks and submitting electronic fingerprints, we vacillated about whether adopting Cade was the right decision for our family. Several times each day my husband and I would check in with each other to see how we were each feeling. Sometimes he was eager to move ahead and I was having doubts, other times it was reversed. Still none of our family or friends knew we were considering such a life change. We owed it to Heidi to tell her as quickly as possible if we decided not to take Cade because she would have to find another placement immediately. Her primary goal was to avoid a temporary placement for Cade. Wherever he landed, she wanted it to be forever because he had already had so many transitions at such a young age.

My daughter, Caity's, fourth birthday was January 12. That evening I sat on the edge of her bed and told her, "Daddy and I have a really important decision to make and we need you to help us. There is a little boy who needs a family and we are trying to decide if he should come and be a part of our family. What would you think of that?"

"I think I would be sad."

"Really? Why?"

"Because I like being alone!" This was probably not a surprising response from a four-year-old who had always been an only child. I explained that I understood, but there would be times when she could still be alone with Mama or Daddy. Cade could go with the other parent. I said that she and I could still go to the grocery store together—her favorite activity. Caity perked up and said, "If we went to the grocery, he could ride in the cart and I could walk alongside!" I agreed and added, "If we got one of the carts that looks like a car, you could show him how to drive. He's only two, so he will need you to show him lots of things."

"Okay, I'm not sad anymore," she said with finality. I waited a few minutes and tried to bring it up again and she said, "Mama, I told you. I'm not sad anymore."

That evening, I had a revelation. It finally occurred to me that by adopting me, my dad had made my life better. In 1964, when I was born, my mother would have struggled, financially and socially, as a single parent. Wasn't this my chance to pay back the life-changing favor I'd been given? Was that why this opportunity had been presented to us? Suddenly I knew what our decision had to be.

We still hadn't shared our decision with our family and friends. The situation became more urgent the next day when Caity started announcing to anyone who would listen, "I'm getting a brother and he's two!" The way she explained it, there was a little boy who needed a warm bed and we had an extra bedroom.

Over the next couple of weeks, we worked with the foster family to execute a transition plan to move our son to our home permanently. When we initially met the foster parents, I had to remind myself that they were not bad people. After all, they had taken Cade to begin with. I needed to trust that they had legitimate reasons for not adopting.

The foster mom was in her mid-thirties. She seemed downright bubbly—and stressed out. "We just took him for a little while to help out." She explained that she had two other children—another two-year-old and a four-year-old. As she spoke, I had the sense that she was struggling to manage three young children—two of whom were in diapers. I couldn't judge her. She told us that Cade liked meat and goldfish crackers. He liked to sleep with his stuffed bunny and really enjoyed playing with his plastic dinosaur collection.

When women at the Bean Project talked about social workers who'd taken their kids, they always painted themselves as victims who had unwittingly lost their children and the social workers as villains who took their children away. But my experience as a newly adoptive mother was that social workers worked tirelessly and compassionately to ensure the safety and security of children.

Cade became a part of our family on February 5, seven weeks after I first heard about him from Marie. The first night we took him upstairs to his bedroom, the four of us sat on the floor and rolled a ball to each other. After a few rolls back and forth, Cade suddenly stood and walked directly to Bill and gave him a kiss. It was a sweet moment, made more tender by its spontaneity.

Though we had just begun the six-month waiting period before the adoption would be finalized, for our family, it was already permanent. We created a modified birth announcement to inform friends of Cade's arrival, and I began talking about it at work. Once Cade was officially a part of our family, I wanted to know for sure if we were related. I contacted a cousin who had done some genealogical research on the Heberlein family. She provided me with all of the details I needed to recreate a family tree that showed Cade and I were indeed family. Marie and I were third cousins; our great-grandfathers were brothers. Cade belonged with us.

Secure in the knowledge that we were on our way to finalizing the adoption in six months, I refocused on my job and on getting to know the new women in the program. One day, I sat at the jewelry table where Morgan and a few other women were working. I was just checking in, with no agenda except to get acquainted.

Morgan's blue eyes viewed me cautiously. "I heard you talking about your son that you are adopting. I was wondering about how that all works." Morgan had a soft voice that made her seem young. I told her a little bit and then asked why she was curious.

"Once I am out of the halfway house, I'd like to start working on getting my daughter back."

"Where is she now?" I asked, assuming her child was in foster care awaiting approval to go back to Morgan, like the children of most of the moms I met.

"She's been adopted. They made me sign away my rights before I went to prison."

"She has actually been adopted? I mean, the adoption has been finalized?" I asked, suddenly confused.

"Yes, but I want to get her back. I didn't want to give her up. They made me do it. I didn't understand what it meant when I signed the papers." She went on to tell me more about the circumstances surrounding her addiction and arrest.

She explained how she'd been using meth with the guy she was dating—her daughter's father. The police caught them at a motel. Morgan's boyfriend jumped out a fifth-story window and tried to run from the cops. When he jumped, Morgan stayed in the motel room, with the meth, weapons and all of the equipment they'd been using steal people's identities.

As an adoptive mother, I struggled with my feelings for this young woman. Like Cade's birth mother, she had been pressured to terminate her parental rights when she went to prison. This isn't common; more than two-thirds of children whose parents go to prison are placed with family members. Incarceration per se is not grounds for forced termination of parental rights, but family members can pressure women to relinquish parental rights because of the mother's uncertain future. Other factors are taken into account as well, such as the length of the mother's imprisonment relative to the child's age. Parental rights also may be terminated if there is no apparent safe placement for the child or if the mother has failed to make arrangements prior to her incarceration.

How would I feel if Cade's birth mother came back when released from prison saying that she didn't really mean it, that she didn't understand what she was doing? Perhaps as a trial run for a future birth mother-adoptive mother conversation, I explained to Morgan how I would feel if Cade's birth mother wanted him back when she is released from prison. Morgan listened carefully and said she understood, but repeated that she hadn't realized what she was doing when she signed away her parental rights. Now that she was clean and sober, she realized that it was never what she'd intended.

I felt sympathy for Morgan. After confirming that Morgan's daughter was adopted in an open-adoption county, meaning that the human services department would assist her in contacting her birth mom, I told Morgan what she could expect in terms of contact with her daughter. I also tried to explain what I thought the adoptive mother might be feeling. She likely would try to protect her adoptive daughter, and not want to expose her to Morgan if she wasn't stable. She might resent Morgan for giving up her daughter and then deciding she wanted to see her again. The adoptive mother also might worry that meeting Morgan would confuse the little girl, making her wonder why she had two mothers. What would Morgan say about where she had been and why she had left her daughter?

Morgan plugged away at her goal of contacting her daughter. Eventually, she had her chance to talk on the telephone with the adoptive mother. I coached Morgan on what to say—that she knew she didn't have a good track record, that she was working on making changes and that she hoped one day to have a relationship of some sort with her daughter, but that she knew she had a lot to prove before those things could happen. I told her what I eventually hoped to hear, but still I wondered how I would respond when it was my turn to have this conversation, if that ever came to pass.

As the months went by and Cade settled into our family, he started to exhibit behavioral and emotional problems. The older he got, the less he acted like his peers. By age three, he was frequently aggressive with others, particularly kids who were his "friends." His emotions and physical activity would become escalated and remain escalated for days. During these times, he would eat and sleep very little. At bedtime, after all the usual preparations—bathing, teeth-brushing and reading—he would lie in bed and dismiss us by saying, "Okay, you can go now." He would become violent with babysitters, throwing objects, kicking, and hitting.

My husband and I saw these challenges as a reflection of our parenting skills. This boy had a different temperament from our daughter and we didn't know how to parent him. We consulted a parenting coach, a caring woman named Laura. She had four children—two adopted and two natural—so her perspective was sympathetic. She gave us permission to say we didn't know what we were doing and helped us see that our son's escalating behavior might be caused by a problem he had processing sensory information. Perhaps he was becoming overstimulated and didn't have the skills to address the sensory input he was receiving.

We pursued occupational therapy for over a year, making our son perform seemingly crazy activities such as climbing backwards, belly-down, up flights of stairs; having him sit on my lap facing me, lowering him backwards to the floor then having him pull himself up; racing cotton balls through an obstacle course on the floor using only a straw. These activities were designed to reset his brain and teach him the skills to calm himself when he felt overexcited. The therapy, combined with his improved motor skills as he grew older, did address some of the worst behavioral problems.

But the behavioral and emotional problems weren't over. After fifteen months, we reached a point of diminished returns with the occupational therapy. As Cade approached age five, we wondered how he would function in a classroom environment. We began to see extremely negative behavior. He would act out to hurt others when he perceived that someone was rejecting or criticizing him, or quickly give up whenever he was unsuccessful at something. We often would kick around a soccer ball, only to have Cade kick it across the street the first time he missed it, effectively ending the game for everyone. He showed very little emotion or caring — for himself or others — and showed no empathy or concern for the harm he caused other kids. When he was injured, he didn't show signs pain, such as crying and wanting comfort. He displayed indiscriminate affection for adult women he'd just met, hugging and snuggling into them. He went to extreme, sometimes comical, measures to avoid eye contact. When I talked to him, he would look anywhere but at me. He was impulsive and had no understanding of cause and effect between his actions and the outcome. Our child didn't just have difficulty controlling his body; he showed signs of an inability to integrate into society.

We met Dr. Jane, a psychotherapist, while seeking additional assistance and answers. During our first visit in Dr. Jane's cozy, dimly lit office, we explained why we had come while we watched Cade bounce around the room playing with every toy for a few seconds. Bill and I sat side by side on the couch, telling her Cade's history. Practically on the spot, she made a preliminary diagnosis of Reactive Attachment Disorder (RAD). "I'll need to confirm this, but given what I have observed and what you've told me, I'm pretty sure that is it. This is going to be a long road. We'll know each other for years," she said with a smile. "It's a big burrito, but we'll eat it one bite at a time." She gave us some reading assignments before we left.

As we read the materials Dr. Jane suggested, everything began to come together. RAD is believed to be caused when children experience severe disruptions in their early caregiver relationships. Often, the child is physically or emotionally abused or neglected.

I never thought our son had been abused, but stories that I'd heard from Marie already had convinced me he'd been neglected. She'd described an evening when Cade was about six months old, and he and her daughter were staying with Marie. Marie's daughter was preparing to go out that night, but Cade was fussy. He'd been placed in his infant carrier, which sat in the middle of the floor. As he lay there screaming, his birth mom stepped over him to get to the door. Marie said to her, "Your son is crying. Aren't you going to take care of him?" Her daughter called over her shoulder as she closed the door, "I'll be back in a little while." Her daughter returned two days later. As Marie told me this, it was hard not to imagine a similar scenario in many of the program participants' homes while they were in the midst of their addictions.

As Cade approached five, Dr. Jane helped us recognize that his emotional age was roughly that of a two-year-old. That made sense. I'd learned from a psychologist who sat on our board that when we experience trauma, we tend to get stuck at the emotional level of that time. Later, when new trauma occurs, we revert back to that old sticking point. If this is true, the women in our program haven't developed emotionally beyond adolescence, which is when many of them experienced their first trauma, drug addiction or sexual abuse. Our participants did act like adolescents—gossiping, with little perspective on the larger picture.

My husband and I were not surprised when we reviewed a list of RAD characteristics. We were saddened to realize that our son displayed nearly all of the twenty characteristics on the list, including little impulse control, hyperactive behavior, a preoccupation with blood and gore, and an unwillingness to accept affection. Our frustrations finally had a basis. Consciously and subconsciously, Cade was making it nearly impossible for us to love him. He was trying not to love us, because if he did, we might leave him like all of the other grown-ups in his young life. Once, during a therapy session, Cade said, "I used to be with another family, but they didn't really love me that much, so now I'm with a new family." At three, he already perceived himself as unlovable.

Dr. Jane taught us to be specific with the feedback we gave

Cade. No general statements such as, "You're such a good boy." No blanket comments about how sweet or smart he was. He wouldn't believe it anyway, she warned. Instead, we were to be specific with our feedback, pointing to specific behavior that displayed the characteristic we wanted. He wouldn't be able to believe there was anything good about himself unless we helped him to see evidence of it.

She told us that we'd also need to change our parenting techniques. No more bending down to get to his eye level when we spoke with him. We were establishing our authority as the people in charge. Kids with RAD believe that no adults will take care of them, so they develop the defense mechanism for taking care of themselves and rejecting adult authority. "You can't worry about what other people think," she coached. "From the outside, others will think you're harsh, but this is what's needed." Every time we spoke with Cade, he was to look us in the eye. He was to respond, "Yes, Mama," or "No, Mama." Never, yeah or no. At first, if felt harsh and unnatural to behave this way toward a child, but we quickly saw the difference it made. He began listening to us and acting on our requests. He started wanting to snuggle at bedtime. Cade and I developed a routine in which I'd ask him how many kisses he wanted. He always started with, "A google." Then I'd talk him down to five or ten that I would apply all over his face, ears and neck.

While we were addressing our son's problems, I was still going to work and still participating in morning meetings. In these meetings, I talked about our family's goals for addressing our son's behavior. I occasionally felt angry at Cade's birth mother for the pain she'd caused. Since I couldn't express my anger to her, I directed that anger toward program participants when they talked about the children they'd lost because of addiction or regained custody of after becoming clean. I wanted them to understand the damage they'd done to their kids during their addiction and incarceration. I didn't want the program participants to take for granted their second chance to raise their children. I hoped they understood the responsibility they had to ensure that their kids didn't follow their mother's paths. It was an emotionally messy time for me. Part of me wanted the women to understand the consequences of their addiction and its impact on their kids. And part of me just wanted to focus on making our son better, loving him and helping him learn to love and trust us.

In one Monday morning meeting, I said that I was grateful that the new ADHD medication my son had started taking was working. I said I was so happy for him that he was finally able to calm his body. That afternoon, Agatha stopped me when I walked by her station on the production floor, where she was making a spice mix for Ten Bean Soup. We had met a few weeks earlier when Agatha started working at the Bean. She'd introduced herself in a whisper. "I'm Agatha."

"As in Agatha Christie?" I'd asked, knowing that if I'd heard it right I would easily remember her name. She'd nodded. I noted her smooth ebony skin.

"I love the way you talk about your son," she said.

"Thanks. It's been a tough go since we adopted him."

"Well, I hope my daughter was adopted by a family as good as yours." Agatha went on to explain that she had four daughters and the youngest had been adopted. "My daughters are all grown up now and the three oldest look just like me. I wonder what the youngest looks like."

"How old is she now?"

"She's twenty-one now. She was taken away from me when she was a year old. My mom and I went to pick her up from Human Services. She'd been taken away a few days before because I'd had a dirty U/A. My mom got out of the car to get her, but they saw me in the car and took her away. I was high on crack, and I guess they knew it. Shortly after that I got clean and now I've been clean for twenty years, but I haven't seen her since. I would just like to know how she is. Does she ever wonder about me?"

"And you know she was adopted?"

"Yes, but it was a closed adoption. I'll never be able to find her."

"Do you think she knows she was adopted?" I imagined that since she was so young she might not remember.

"Yes. I think she was adopted by a white family."

"Then, I'm pretty sure she knows," I said. We both chuckled. Then Agatha became serious again.

"I hope she was adopted by a white family."

"Really? Why?" I would have expected that any black woman would want her child to be raised by another black family if she wasn't able to raise the child herself. "Do you think her life would be better by being raised with a white family?"

"Oh, I don't know. I mean, I know there are good white people and bad white people, just like there are good black people and bad black people. But really I hope she was raised by a white family because then she would know she was adopted."

With his curly blond hair and blue eyes, our son looks like he received genes from both my husband and me. We thought this would be a benefit to him since he wouldn't stand out or be forced explain that he was adopted if he didn't want to.

Agatha had an entirely different perspective. "If she knows she was adopted, then maybe someday she'll want to find me. Since it was a closed adoption. I won't ever be able to see her unless she wants to find me."

I told Agatha about our experience as adoptive parents, how we were dealing with the damage done to our son by his birth mom. Everything about these conversations with the program participants—and there were many—left me conflicted between my loyalty to my son and my loyalty toward the women. The more I saw the damage done to my son by his birth mother's neglect and abandonment, the angrier I felt at her.

Our son is improving. We see him experience normal, five-year-old, spontaneous joy more often. He makes friends easily and has begun to show a healthy fear of strangers. Without prompting, he tells me that he loves me. He likes to snuggle, especially when he is hurt or feeling ill. He is intellectually curious and loves asking a question, processing the answer and asking a follow-up question. Dr. Jane said that his progress in just nine months is nearly miraculous.

But we still have our rough days. Cade handles transition poorly and challenges the authority of adults who are new in his world. When he has a new teacher, he is defiant and tries to prove that he is as unlovable as he feels. If he is tired or hungry or overheated, he can have violent outbursts. He still struggles with learning new things—not because he isn't capable, but because he has little belief in himself or his abilities.

Working at the Bean Project has been the best way for me to overcome the feelings of anger and resentment I feel for Cade's birth mother. I likely will never understand addiction and how it can affect one's actions. I do believe that the sober women who arrive at the Bean Project are not the same women they were during their addictions. During their addictions, they were abandoned, strung out and hopeless. They didn't have the capacity to understand how their actions affected their kids. Many grew up in environments similar to what they created for their children, so how is it realistic to expect them to do anything differently? By the time I meet the women of the Bean Project, they are full of possibility. That's what I need to remember about Cade's birth mother. She, too, is full of possibility.

Instead of hoping that we never meet Cade's birth mother, I need to hope for her recovery. Like all of the women who come to the Bean to change their lives, I need to believe in Cade's birth mother's ability to create a new, productive life for herself. When she has done that, she will be in the best position to meet her child. That meeting will not diminish the fact that I also am his mother and love him, nor will it diminish his love for me.

I hope that Cade will someday meet his birth mother, that he will see some of himself in her and that he will be comfortable with that awareness. I know that if he decides he wants to meet her, the best we can do is facilitate that meeting. I never want him to wonder what she is like, what traits he inherited from her, or how her life turned out. In the meantime, our job as parents to this beautiful boy is to make him feel loved, help him discover his unique gifts and create a home that provides security and structure.

NOW WHAT?

In May 2013, I was the co-emcee at the Social Enterprise Alliance National Summit in Minneapolis. I had the opportunity to talk with many of the conference speakers, including Mark Ritchie, Secretary of State of Minnesota. Secretary Ritchie is a strong proponent of social enterprise and was bullish about the potential for nonprofits to earn money by running businesses. During one of our conversations, we talked about how he was championing educational programs in Minnesota's prison system to provide felons with the opportunity to build the skills needed to start a business when they are released from prison. He acknowledged that, because of their felony convictions, they would have difficulty finding jobs with traditional employers. This strategy would help them to create their own employment upon release. We briefly discussed the kinds of businesses felons could start. One example that stood out was cosmetology. I commented that in Colorado, women can take cosmetology classes while they are in prison, but they are not allowed to get the license when they are released. Mr.

Ritchie gave me a puzzled look and said, "Well, that's just a rule. You could get that changed."

The interaction made me realize that we too often look at a problem and accept it for what it is, rather than recognize that we each have the ability to affect change if we choose. In this book, I have presented many of the problems with our systems and social norms. At this point, I'd like to discuss strategies to address those problems.

Here is a list of ten things we can do to create change or support marginalized people in your community:

1. Support sentencing reform to keep more families together. Again and again I've witnessed women whose lives were completely turned around because their addictions led to their arrest and felony conviction. In the past few years changes in sentencing laws have decreased the sentencing disparities that inordinately affect poor people of color, but there is more work to be done. In addition to the changes in sentencing policy, experiences while in prison, the damage done to families of incarcerated individuals, and society's disenfranchisement of felons all need to be addressed. The Sentencing Project, conducting research and advocacy for sentencing reform, provides guidance for how to get involved in changing our criminal justice system that is negatively affecting our poor communities. Visit www.thesentencingproject.org for more information.

2. Foster or adopt a child from the United States. My family's experience was unique. We hadn't investigated adoption before we started our journey, so my only experience with adoption—besides my own—was observing my friends who adopted internationally. Once, a program participant described the great experience she had with her foster family. She was placed there

while her mother was in rehab and it was the only time in her life that she had a fatherly role model. She fondly remembered the normalcy she felt while she was placed with that foster family.

There are many children in the United States who are in the foster care who will eventually need a new family. In 2002, over 51,000 kids were adopted from foster care. These kids tend to be older—the largest percentage of foster-to-adopt kids fall into the one-to-five-year-old range, while almost all international adoptions are completed before the child is four years old. Adopting older kids can be challenging, but it strikes me as extremely sad to allow a child to age out of the foster care system at age eighteen without ever having had a family.

3. Become a Big Brother or Big Sister. Even if you are unable to foster or adopt a child, many children need mentors. Big Brothers Big Sisters is a community-based mentoring program that matches youth from low-income backgrounds with adult volunteers who agree to spend time together each week. There are hundreds of Big Brothers Big Sisters agencies across the country. Visit www.bbbs.org for more information about getting involved.

I firmly believe that if you can change a woman's life, you can change her family's life, but sometimes a mother needs additional support while she is working to bring income to the family. Many women have told me they lacked role models while they were growing up. Big brothers and big sisters provide an opportunity for consistency and companionship.

The Coalition for Evidence-Based Policy, a nonprofit, nonpartisan organization, found that youth who participated in the Big Brothers Big Sisters program were less likely to have started using illegal drugs or alcohol, skipped fewer days of school and had slightly higher GPAs.

4. Hire a felon or someone who is trying to move off welfare assistance. The Work Opportunity Tax Credit provides tax credit on federal taxes for each qualified hire. The amount of tax credit is based on wages. Qualified hires include veterans, those moving from welfare to work, felons and employees who are disabled. More information can be found with the U.S. Department of Labor. Visit www.doleta.gov/business/incentives/opptax/.

5. Support a women's foundation in your area. Women's foundations work on issues important to women, such as welfare reform and equal pay. A quick internet search can yield foundations in your community that support women's issues and policy reform.

6. Give where you live. Community foundations address issues that are important to the community. Find a community foundation near you by visiting the Council on Foundations' community foundation locator: www.cof.org.

7. Keep an open mind. Perhaps one of the biggest lessons I've learned is that my attitudes and opinions about others are not necessarily correct, they are merely shaped by my experiences and background. As such, I've learned to be open to other ideas, attitudes and opinions. I may not change my mind, but I may allow myself to see things differently. I've realized there is benefit to being open-minded. It's sure a lot more fun. Judgment is one of the biggest barriers preventing marginalized people in our communities from changing their lives. Don't assume you know about why someone is homeless, addicted or a felon. Get involved with local nonprofit organizations that serve these populations to get the real story.

8. Let addicts fail or succeed on their own. If there is an addict in your life, help connect them to rehabilitation resources such as Alcoholics Anonymous or Narcotics Anonymous. Then get out of their way and let them succeed or fail. The responsibility for getting and staying clean can rest only with the addict, and

to the extent we try to help, I believe we are enabling further addiction. Consider going to Al-Anon, a support group designed for families of alcoholics or addicts.

9. Support safe houses. Too many women are unable to leave abusive relationship because they have nowhere else to go. There are far too few beds for women trying to escape abuse and even fewer places where women can go with their kids. As members of communities where abuse exists—as it exists in all of our communities—we can help by giving our time and treasure to support local safe houses so that they are available for battered women and children when needed.

10. Start a social enterprise. I believe that work is the best way to teach someone how to work. Many existing nonprofit organizations that teach men and women job readiness skills would welcome assistance. Or start your own social enterprise. Visit the Social Enterprise Alliance website for resources (www. se-alliance.org). For more information about the Campaign to Cut Poverty in Half in Ten Years, visit halfinten.org/get_involved. Sign the pledge and learn how you can get involved.

Acknowledgements

I must start by thanking my husband, Bill. He's my greatest advocate and president of my fan club. Without his support I wouldn't have been able to carve out the time necessary to write a book. He never doubted me and never pressured me to complete the project.

While writing this book, I've met many great writers whose work I admire. Chief among them is my mentor and friend Shari Caudron, who helped me navigate the process of bringing this book to fruition. With tough love, she pushed me to make this the best book it could be. She brought to the table my editor, Peter Lewis, and line editor, Rebecca Berg. Shari, Pete and Rebecca made me appear to be a much better writer than I could have on my own. I appreciate Cindi Yaklich's design work. She was able to create an image that perfectly depicted what I could only express in words. I also thank Lighthouse Writer's Workshop for creating a haven for writers of all creeds. It was fantastic to have a community when I started on this very solitary journey.

The staff members of Women's Bean Project have provided a terrific sounding board. They've been willing to reminisce and commiserate when I wanted to discuss one woman or another. Special thanks go to Geoff Lucas and Bob Macdonald who have been teammates throughout my entire journey at the Bean Project. I am appreciative beyond words for everything they have contributed to Women's Bean Project. All of the staff members, past and present, deserve thanks for their commitment to the cause and their willingness to press for continuous improvement in the name of the mission.

Many dedicated volunteers have given their time, talent and treasure throughout the Bean Project's history. Years ago someone told me, "Every executive gets the board she deserves." I hope this is true because I have been fortunate to know many talented, smart and committed board members—many of whom have become dear friends. I owe a debt of gratitude to Susan Powers, Judith Gomez and Peggy Driscoll for deciding I was the right person to hire for this job.

Most importantly, I want to express my admiration for the women who arrive at the Bean Project with a dream for a better life. I thank them for their willingness to help me tell their stories and hope I have done them justice.

ABOUT THE AUTHOR

TAMRA RYAN draws from more than 20 years of marketing and sales experience as the CEO of the Women's Bean Project, bringing a business-savvy side to the nationally-recognized social enterprise. Using a hands-on approach, she has successfully built a culture that caters to women attempting to break the cycle of chronic unemployment and poverty. Ms. Ryan's role within the non-profit focuses on leading a team of professionals in the implementation of business strategy, including program and operational expansion to increase the Bean Project's impact on the community.

She is the recipient of numerous awards, including the Judith M. Kaufmann award for Civic Entrepreneurship, presented by The Denver Foundation; Regis University's Social Entrepreneurship Award; and Outstanding Alumnus, presented by the Colorado Leadership Alliance in 2006; and a Circles of Change Award winner in 2013. In 2012 she was named one of Colorado's up and coming most influential women by The Denver Post. Ms. Ryan is also the board chair for the Colorado Chapter of the Social Enterprise Alliance. She was a speaker at TEDxMilehigh in June, 2013.